9

Editor, English-language edition: Ellen Nidy
Translated from the French by
Alexandra Bonfante-Warren and Molly Stevens

Library of Congress Control Number: 2001098143

ISBN 0-8109-0565-5

This book was produced by Atalante/Paris-éditions
for Éditions de La Martinière.

Printed and bound in Italy
10 9 8 7 6 5 4 3 2 1

Harry N. Abrams, Inc.
100 Fifth Avenue
New York, N.Y. 10011
www.abramsbooks.com

Abrams is a subsidiary of

LA MARTINIÈRE
GROUPE

David Teboul

Yves Saint Laurent
5, avenue Marceau
75116 Paris
France

Harry N. Abrams, Inc., Publishers

Foreword by
Pierre Bergé

What if, just for once, I didn't talk about Yves Saint Laurent? If as a commentary on these photographs I spoke of that unknown, mysterious world that has surrounded him for so many years? In reality, a couture house resembles nothing so much as a beehive, with its workers, warriors, watchers, and artisans, whose only purpose is to hatch the precious eggs that, in our trade, are called the collections. Yes, a beehive, one that for years now has hummed so loudly that it can be heard in the four corners of the earth. In the beginning is the *sketch*. That's our *Word*. That is what leads, what remains the referent. Then, there is the *pattern*, which allows assessment, interruption, continuity. Then, the *fabric*, which marks an essential stage, the stage of boldness and risk. Finally, the *model* arrives, which takes its first tentative steps before joining the others, to form the *collection*. Although overcoming all these trials requires goodwill on everyone's part, this goodwill would be nothing without talent. Because that's really what it's all about. This hive—our couture house—is a-buzz with talent. At every stage, they appear, expand, and echo one another. Have they said that we're proud of one another? That we love one another? That we speak the same language? This Esperanto that we have forged allows us to recognize one another and to smile at the accents of others. Everyone mobilizes their will, tightens their muscles toward a single end: *the collection* that will be shown at a certain hour on a certain day. Then all the fatigue and all the effort are forgotten. The garments have been taken up to the baptismal fonts. They have been received by the public, will live their lives, no longer belong to us.

That's when we restore our strength, in shadows and in silence, ready our arms for new battles. Once again, it will be the *sketch*, the *pattern*, the *fabric*, the *model*, the *collection*. We know this story very well: we have been telling it for forty years. And yet, it continues to surprise and enthrall us. As if we didn't know the ending.

Pierre Bergé

Text by
David Teboul

How insignificant, at the moment, seem the influences of the sensible things which
are tossed and fall and lie about us, so, or so, in the environment of early childhood.
How indelibly, as we afterwards discover, they affect us; with what capricious attractions
and associations they figure themselves on the white paper, the smooth wax, of our
ingenuous souls, as "with lead in the rock for ever," giving form and feature, and as it
were assigned house-room in our memory, to early experiences of feeling and thought,
which abide with us ever afterwards, thus, and not otherwise. The realities and passion,
the rumours of the greater world without, steal in upon us, each by its own special little
passage-way, through the wall of custom about us; and never afterwards quite detach
themselves from this or that accident, or trick, in the mode of their first entrance to us.
Our susceptibilities, the discovery of our powers, manifold experiences — our various
experiences of the coming and going of bodily pain, for instance — belong to this or
the other well-remembered place in the material habitation — that little white room
with the window across which the heavy blossoms could beat so peevishly in the wind,
with just that particular catch or throb, such a sense of teasing in it, on gusty mornings.

Walter Pater, "The Child in the House," 1887

Every social level has its own attraction. It can be just as interesting for the artist
to depict the manners of a queen as the habits of a dressmaker.

Marcel Proust

Like Scott Fitzgerald, I adore mortal frenzy. I love Visconti and troubled times like
those in Senso. *Decadence attracts me. It heralds a new world. I find the vision*
of a society in combat, torn between life and death, magnificent .

From *Yves Saint Laurent* by Laurence Benaïm, 1993

Last November, the doors of 5 avenue Marceau opened onto a secret place: the house of the master Yves Saint Laurent. For three months we were able to shut ourselves up in this Napoleon III–style townhouse in the heart of Paris's best neighborhood and given the freedom to make the film we wished to make. In a world of mirrors and negotiated flurries, of punctilious tensions and light touches, we discovered an entire tribe of dressmakers and tradesmen, embroiderers and workroom managers, all animating, day after day, this theater of the ephemeral with its enchantments. This is not a company, but a *house*— you could even say a *bottega*, a shop of Renaissance Florence—where the curtain rises every morning on a ritual involving almost two hundred participants engaged head over heels in a meditation that is both magical and material.

My childhood took place surrounded by women who read *Elle*. In the magazine, they said that Yves Saint Laurent was not only a couturier but a secret figure, and so I have always considered him more a character of fiction than of the fashion world. When he turned his back on the conventions of the slightly colorless colonial bourgeoisie, he was obliged to reinvent himself, trusting only to Ariadne's thread of his childhood dreams. He was, in fact, not yet fourteen years old when he predicted to his flabbergasted family circle that his name "would one day shine in gold letters on the Champs-Élysées." Initially, then, there was the Oran of before the Algerian war, a sweet, maternal wellspring, encapsulated within one simple image: the child cutting squares of fabric out of his mother's dresses to make clothes for his doll-models. What a scissors cut can reveal! By means of this private breach, little Saint Laurent merged reality and manner. With this daring, transgressive gesture, he intuitively announced who he was, and by the same token opened the mystery of eros to the light of day. Only a child could have pulled off such a loving coup—and not just any child. In 1957, the young native of Oran arrived in the capital, already knowing who the major players were from the Parisian magazines' society columns. The excellent sponsorship of a few inspired mentors—Michel de Brunhoff, then Pierre Bergé— guided him in his conquest of a world in which women were still merely luxury display units for couture's great names. In no time, he was with Christian Dior's house, where he shone. And when Dior died, it was Saint Laurent who was named to succeed him—at twenty-one years old! All doors immediately opened. Within a few months, he had position and reputation. He could have been satisfied with that, settled down, agreed to occupy a prominent place in a vainglorious social order. It was a prewar holdover, this view of the couturier as an artist-costumer. The couturier was expected to contribute his savoir-faire to the elaboration and refinement of the codes of a complex way of life: balls, dress rehearsals at the opera, seasons on the Côte d'azur. This was haute couture, and it reached its peak in the 1930s. But the war delivered this way of life a deathblow—although no one realized it yet. Something ended with Dior—and something else began: fashion, the site of social representation, had reached the street.

Yves Saint Laurent moved within this new configuration armed with nothing but his style and his ability to shape and construct it. He owed this crucial asset to the female family environment he came from and to an assiduous immersion in fashion magazines. During his formative years, he honed both his intuition and his technical skills in his work with artisans, so that by the time he arrived in Paris, he was skilled in the various disciplines of fashion. All that remained was for him to work out and implement his own individual means of expression. On the one hand was his childhood, on the other was the outside world; that is fashion, the stereotypical store informed by indifference. To find his way there, he had, in a sense, to renounce elegance. Yves Saint Laurent understood early on that elegance is not an end in itself—and forty years later, twice a year, this credo resounds when he presents his couture collections. Because a collection is a gesture, a sign, a bow before turning away and saying goodbye. In this regard, Yves Saint Laurent is spiritually akin to Jean-Michel Frank, a 1930s decorator, a man of line and blueprint, who always announced on finishing an apartment, "That's it. Now you can start ruining it!"

Saint Laurent's ambivalence lies in his being at one and the same time in the sublime and on the dark side, the leather, the drugs, the sexual behavior. Therein is his magic. Like Proust's Swann, he contains both sides. His is the way of androgyny and femininity. He is dark, exuberant, extravagant—and anxious. Number 5 avenue Marceau is a refined, chic, Viscontian place—by no means a site for sordid encounters. And yet I sense the flip-side of this decor, a place that is not sinister in itself, but where I imagine one may play-act at such things. The history of this house is of two young men who meet. One of them, Pierre Bergé, is a teacher's son, father dead, born in Île d'Oléron; the other, Yves Saint Laurent, is from Oran, son of the solid colonial middle class of the time. But when he arrived in France, he was no longer anything.

So at first both of them were sort of outsiders and both were out to conquer the world. The conformists, the proper ones, operate very differently. They reproduce, insure, make something of their lives. Saint Laurent, on the other hand, is dedicated to his art. His taste for the sinister, the sublime, the perfect, obsessive arrangement of the beautiful was only the backdrop of his passionate ambition to rock the fashion establishment. Very early on, he went over to the women's side. But since he is homosexual, his incapacity to desire women and his intimate promiscuity with them emerge as a sublimation of an impossible love. There is in fashion, and especially in haute couture, something that exists outside reality: a dream, a wild idealization.

Saint Laurent has always had the boldness of a pariah, a defector, which inspires unexpected gestures, small shifts, and tiny subversions of the code, which in turn causes transfiguring beauty to suddenly burst forth. A vocabulary may be simple, but if it is extraordinary it becomes a language. Saint Laurent is not an abstractionist, but a figurative artist. In his work, we find Matisse and his *Voyage au Maroc*, the discovery of color.

It is as if Matisse passed his palette on to the couturier. Balthus is present as well in the drawings, in the languid *maniera* and the poses that give the lie to the gaze. At the same time, creative intelligence cannot be described by a formal equation. It must have a certain inclination (made up of little tricks and many gimmicks—that's what's called the gaze) toward appropriating social codes, anticipating the overturning of conventions, and formulating collective aspirations.

From the postwar period on, many talented couturiers have designed outstanding clothing. Only two, however, have really stood out: Mademoiselle Chanel—who gave women their freedom—and Yves Saint Laurent—who gave them their power. He understood very early on that men's clothes were both adapted to their power and signifiers of it. So he took men's clothes and transformed them to dress women in them. He didn't disguise women as men, but simply used clothing's code to enable women to feel different. This revolution was called *pant suit, tuxedo, trench coat, bush shirt, pea-coat*. Before Saint Laurent, women didn't wear pants, and their clothes had no pockets: their fragility was encoded. With him, they symbolically took over—before acquiring power in real life. His work as couturier went in tandem with the woman's revolution.

At the same time, it is not that simple. For Saint Laurent also—madly—loves fragile women, evening dresses, embroidery, all that goes toward creating a certain kind of eternal feminine. Yves Saint Laurent's intuitions and sensibilities are paradoxical. He took whatever he found—such as men's clothing—and transformed it. He achieved a sort of rewriting. In my mind, that is what genius is. Because no one had thought of displacing this small, existing thing. It took a pariah to do it, someone coming from outside.

Catherine Deneuve said this about it: "Yves Saint Laurent designs for women who lead double lives. During the day, his clothes help us face a world full of strangers. They allow us to go everywhere without attracting attention, and their somewhat masculine look gives us the strength to stand up to encounters that can become confrontational. In the evening, when we go back to the people we are close to, they help us look seductive." Collection after collection, the couturier's style reaffirms this principle of ambivalence. His personal rules support this idea. Far from being fixed in the appearance of "creatures," his women are sudden, furtive apparitions. Their clothes are not costumes but moments of a metamorphosis. Androgyny, therefore, not as lack of differentiation, but as a re-enchantment of the game of gender: Woman is multiple, as she alone knows how to be—the opposite of the man-male fixed in a single, often dominant posture. This is why Yves Saint Laurent's world is not unisex, whatever they may say. It is eroticism, because the garment must not clothe, but reveal. This revealing, this *glamour*, is the empyrean of being. Seductiveness—the constant in the turbulence of genders—blossoms in the half-light of transparency. So this couturier sent into orbit certain essential paradoxes concerning our ideas about clothing, thereby creating a remarkable figure, a modern heroine: a woman who is neither mother nor working girl, neither slut nor slave. She is, by turns, all of these—and none. Free, because she is shifting. That is what makes Yves Saint Laurent's women desirable. She is an absolutely contemporary type of the eternal feminine, a splendid, gentle, and elusive incarnation. She is one of the filmmaker Jacques Demy's girls, confounding expectations and evading the traps of the game of love. Such a girl, far from being a creature "as beautiful as a dream of stone," is an utterly seductive being, who appears to mortal eyes, depending upon the time of day, as elf, sylph, or passerby.

There is a certain kind of knowledge—the purview of those rare few able to discern emerging designs, future forms, the crowd's innate propositions—whose source derives from experience of the world. How many sensitive abductions, unexpected ravishments are to be put down to Yves Saint Laurent, to the man who stole so much from the street, only to return everything as timeless shapes? When we enter 5 avenue Marceau, the threads of fiction stretch. The House is the last to maintain the tradition of apprenticeship. Everything is done here. An article of clothing often requires more than one hundred hours' work; the manufacturing stages are extremely precise: a sketch, the creation of the pattern—the leno model of what will be a dress or a suit—on a wooden mannequin, a paper pattern to correct the lines, the mounting of the leno, the molding of the jacket and attaching of the sleeves, the choice of fabrics, repeated fittings on live models, the finals checks. All these steps are required rituals for every piece of clothing in the collection. This organization of the work answers not to any economic rationale, but to an organic principle that joins, in a single gesture, Yves Saint Laurent and his workshops. It looks like love—and it is. The poet's true home is his atelier, which both contains the world and protects him from it. At 5 avenue Marceau, I traveled as if adopted into the land of childhood. Eroticism is, in a way, the other side of childhood—humanity's childhood, of course, as Aristophanes described it in Plato's *Symposium*: "Besides the two sexes, male and female, which we have at present, there was a third which partook of both, and for which we still have a name." The act of creation in couture gives flesh to this phantasm. In the beginning, there is only the idea, the moment: a pencil stroke delivered to the atelier's foremen and -women. Gradually, the hand-to-hand takes shape. The grace achieved by the couturier's suffering is realized by the design on the runway. On the one hand there is the elaboration that proceeds by slow adjustments and measured audacities, on the other, there is the stunning effect of its passage onto a platform. With a certain taste for abandonment, Saint Laurent always withdraws at the last moment before the presentation to the public in order to remain in the phantasm he has long borne within himself and finally delivered in the form of a female "other." Therein may lie the deep turbulence that is the source of the couturier's work. Yves Saint Laurent's creations are women that only the gaze can capture; they appear not in the realm of the real but in the domain of desire. They are sometimes exuberant expressions of love, in which the sublimation of the body appears as the inevitable horizon of an obsessive quest for beauty: "All this to-do is a relic of that original state of ours, when we were whole; and now, when we are longing for and following after that primeval wholeness, we say we are in love." Aristophanes again. But Yves Saint Laurent has also been an exterior man. He went out into the world and pursued a good many of its excesses. More than some others, he has known the tumult, sought it. Thrown himself publicly into it. With some, ambiguity is a pose—with others, a vertiginous vitality. As a homosexual, Yves Saint Laurent knows the importance of appearance and the need to play with it, he knows how to multiply his personalities in order to thwart allegiances. His ability to idealize, which keeps him so firmly apart from "fashion," could have made him the couturier of the valiant women of the ancient alliance—Judith, Deborah, and Esther—strong, political heroines, builders of destinies, figures of rejoicing. At the same time, however, he appropriates leather jackets to clothe his deities.

When he invented ready-to-wear in 1966, it was not to open shop windows onto the street, or to participate in a collective movement toward standardization. Neither his first shop, in Saint-Germain, nor any of the others that he would open all over the world, was intended to display panoplies designed to dress the sumptuary icons of a promoted way of life. His ready-to-wear boutiques allow the mystery that is Yves Saint Laurent to be sensed at a glance: he does not create clothing, he creates a style. If this were not the case, yesterday's and today's *couturasses*—or the hacks, a word he coined to describe those who serenely profit from the decline of taste—would have easily copied and adapted the master's "recipes" to the trend *du jour*. But that hasn't happened. Yves Saint Laurent has no heir. In these times governed by the mystique of plenty, of profusion disguised as asceticism—whether Japanese or Anglo-Saxon—Yves Saint Laurent adheres to no system. He does not believe that clothes make the man. He has only successors, and no lack of acknowledgment.

Here is a man alone, of a stature recalling Gary Cooper's. Is he a star? Yes—but what a word to describe this monument of interiority! The beauty he offers is a presence so inhabited by silence as to become haunting. For, when almost twenty years ago, in 1983, excess and parties became obligatory and regimented, Yves Saint Laurent, like a Proustian hero, abandoned the world to dedicate himself exclusively to couture, as if to a private walkabout. His retreat is evidence of a feeling, a sign, a need. There is nothing very unusual about the aspiration to be only that, to be all in all to oneself, but there are very few of those converts or hermits who dare to go for the radical renunciation, agreeing to take on the difficulty it implies: to remain forever and relentlessly with oneself.

For some time now, Yves Saint Laurent has been living apart from the present, with his body of work as his only companion. In the end, can we see him otherwise than in the imperfect tense? This is the challenge and the privilege offered the filmmaker: to record what is no more, what has no (or no longer) reason to exist, to show the present of a past.

Christian Baute
presents

a
Movimento Production
Canal +
Transatlantic Video
production

with the participation of
Westdeutscher Rundfunk Köln

Yves Saint Laurent
5, avenue Marceau
75116 Paris
France

A film by
David Teboul

writer and director
David Teboul

director of photography
Caroline Champetier
assistant
Léo Hinstin

sound
Laurent Malan

editing
Martine Giordano
assistant
Patric Chiha

sound editing
Fabien Krzyzanowski
mixing
Olivier Dohut
sound effects
Laurent Lévy

picture editor
James A. Fox
assistant
Patric Chiha

executive producer
Frédéric Luzy

with the exceptional participation of
Catherine Deneuve

with
Yves Saint Laurent
Pierre Bergé
Anne-Marie Muñoz
Loulou de la Falaise
Hélène de Ludinghausen

and the **Studio**

and the participation of
Laëtitia Casta

with
Georgette Capelli
Colette Maciet
Christelle Posada
Frédérique Desinde
Marie-Thérèse Herzog
Jean-Pierre Derbord
Philippe Lesage
Alain Marchais

and all the ateliers

and
Christian Forel
and his team

It all starts with a sketch. Yves Saint Laurent goes away to draw, often to Marrakech. At first, it's only an intuition. He doesn't even know how it happens himself, but, at some point, his hand draws a line. He draws one, ten, a hundred sketches. When he stops, the collection is before him. The preliminaries of the collection, its spirit, but also many very precise details are already there. Upon his return to Paris, he calls in his studio supervisors and lays the sketches before them. Madame Colette and Madame Georgette are responsible for the dresses; Monsieur Jean-Pierre and Monsieur Alain are in charge of suits. Understanding the sketches is what counts. They take a look at them and choose. Saint Laurent steps in. He knows his studio: how one sketch will be good for a particular person's intuition, how another will match another's talent. With the large sheets rolled under their arms, the supervisors go back to their own studios and distribute the drawings to the workers. They get to work under the watch of their supervisors who give them directions as they go. This is how they make what is called a pattern; that is, the first form of the dress or suit. The pattern moves, because movement was already in the drawing. It's a story without words. Only a few words are needed. Yves Saint Laurent doesn't expect his studio to do a job, but to interpret a changing, silent message. For what is important in the end is the expression of the piece.

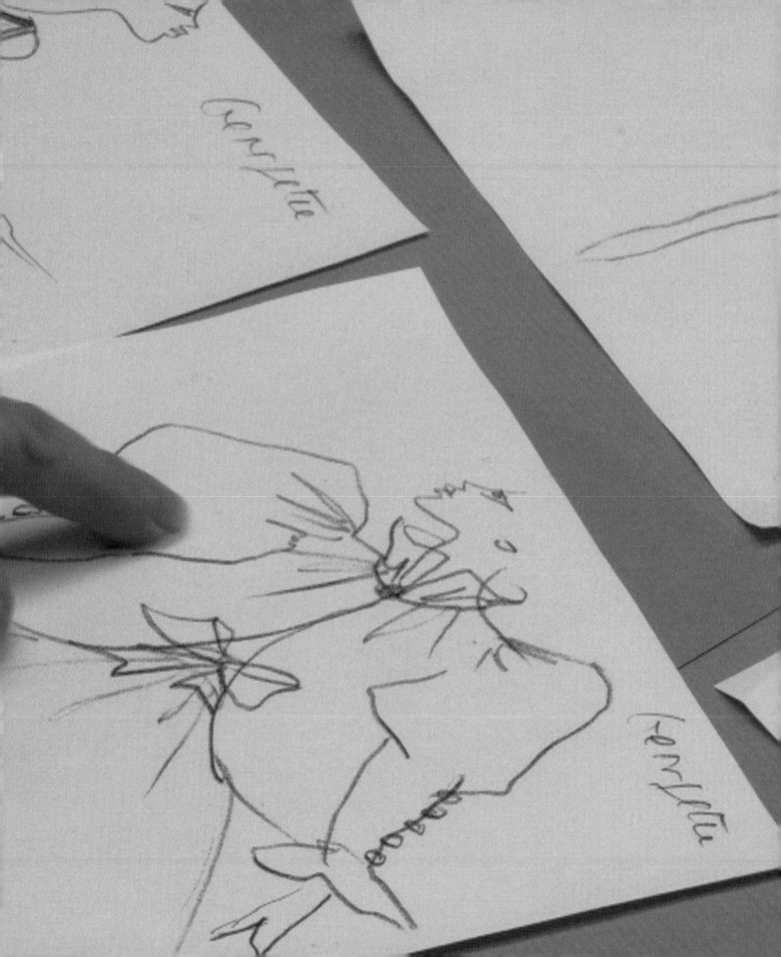

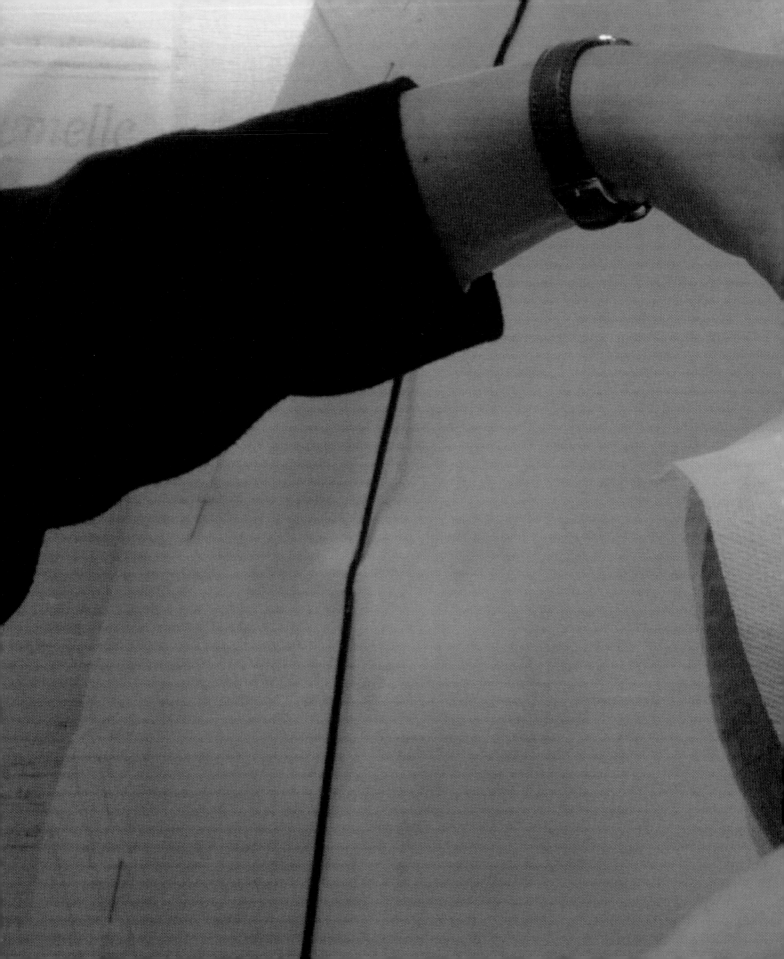

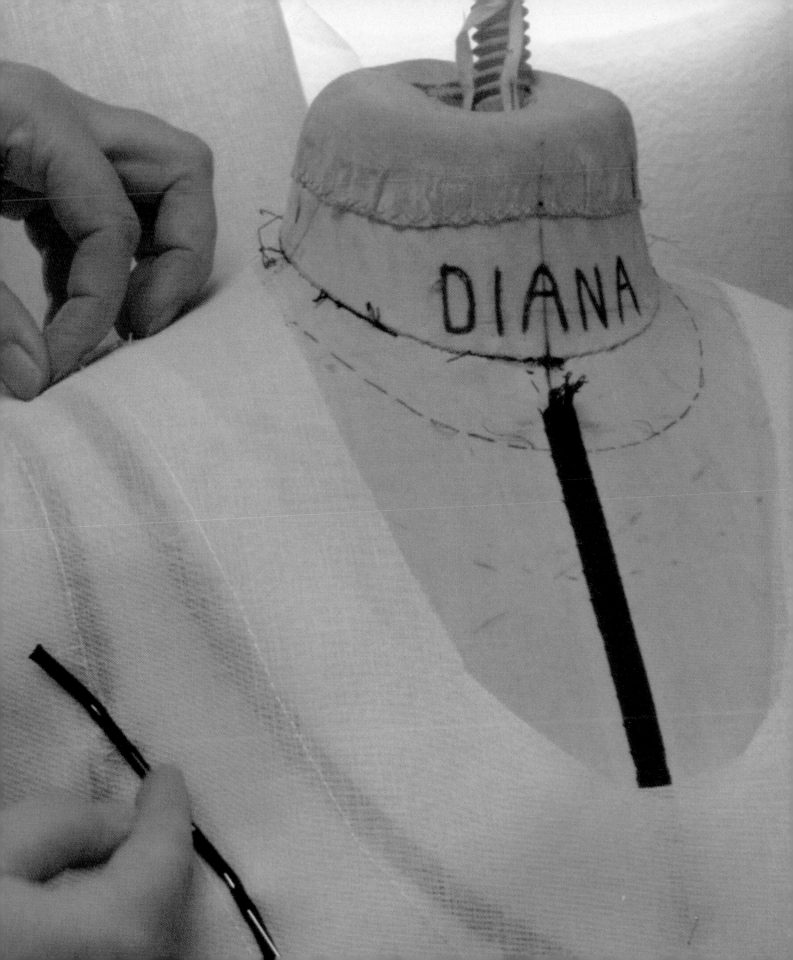

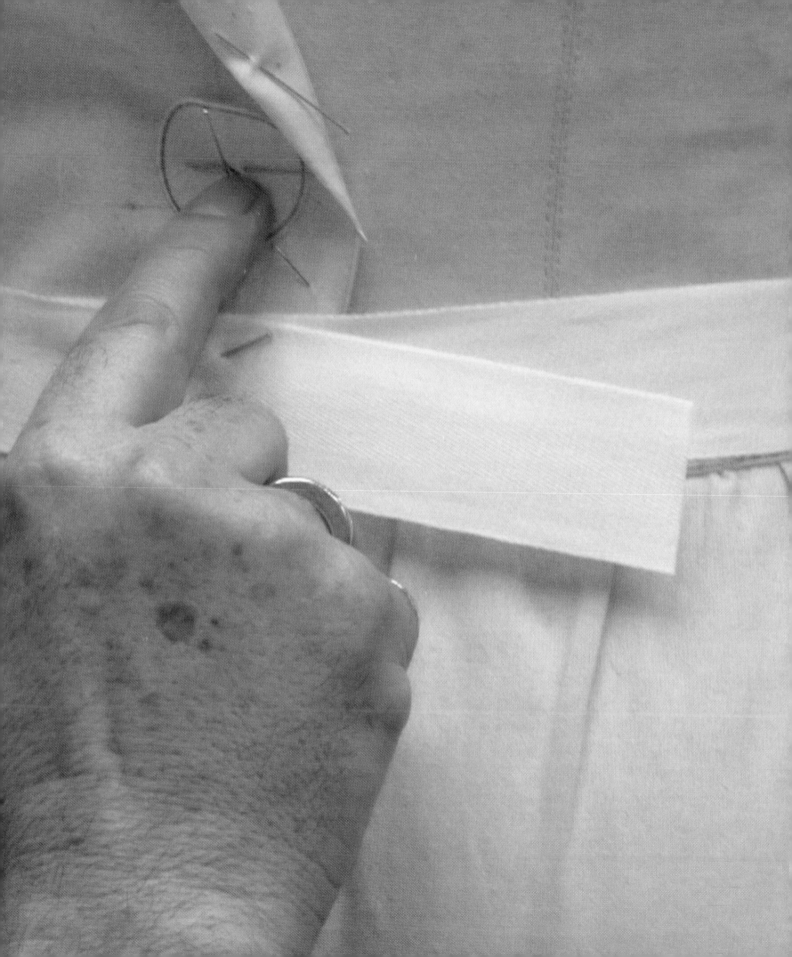

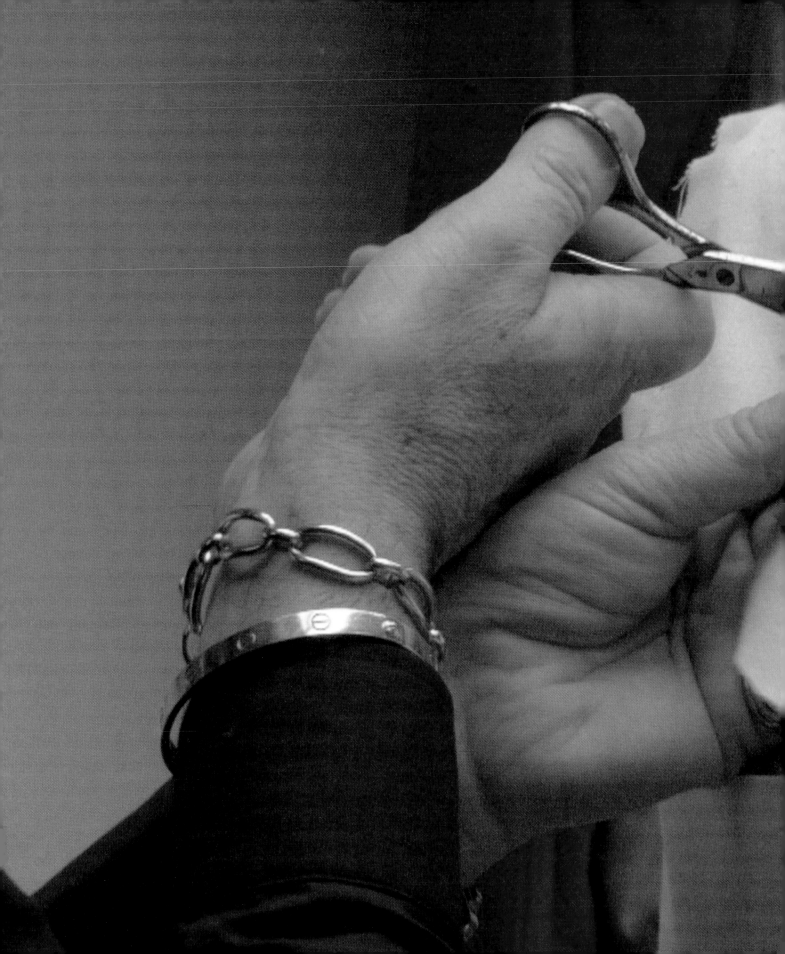

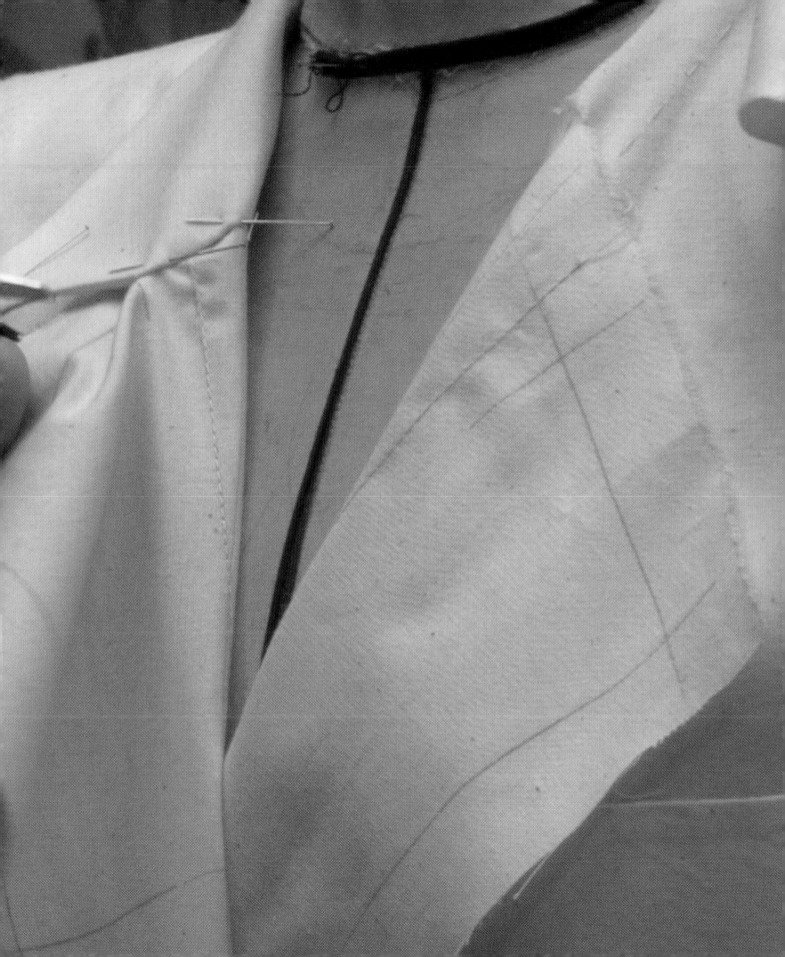

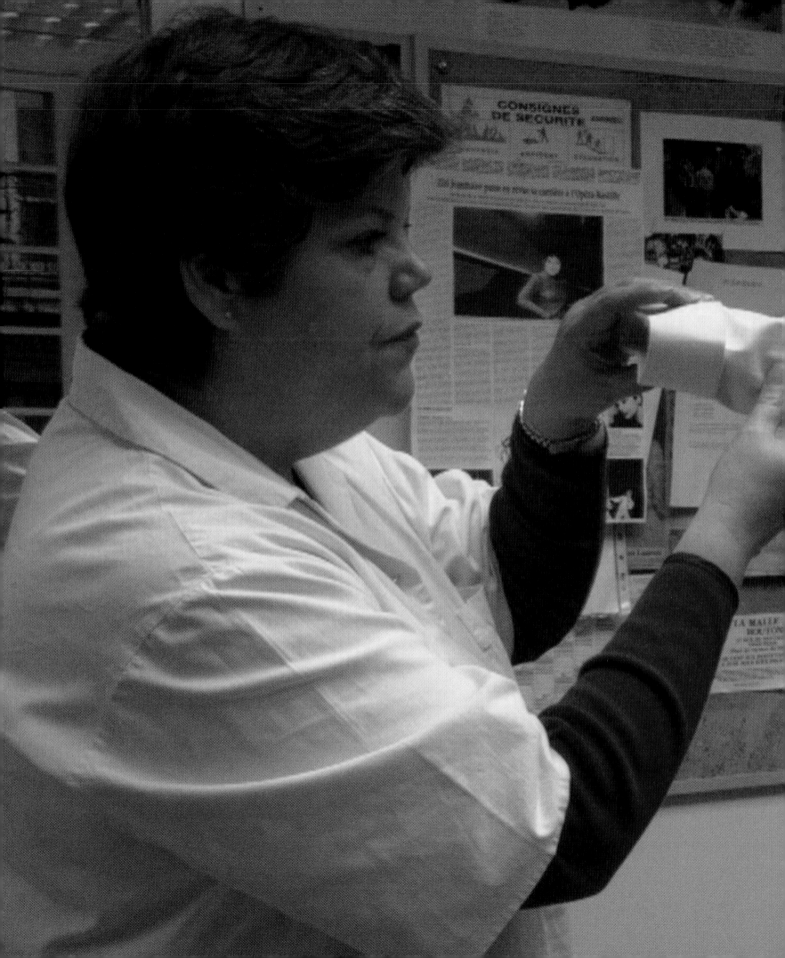

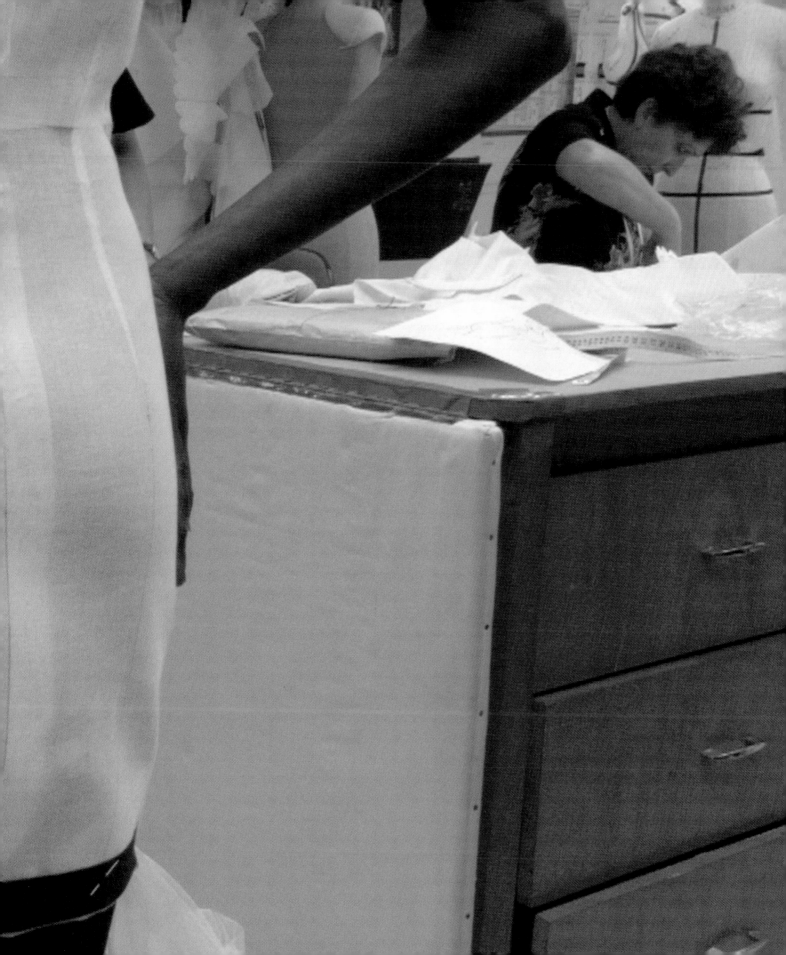

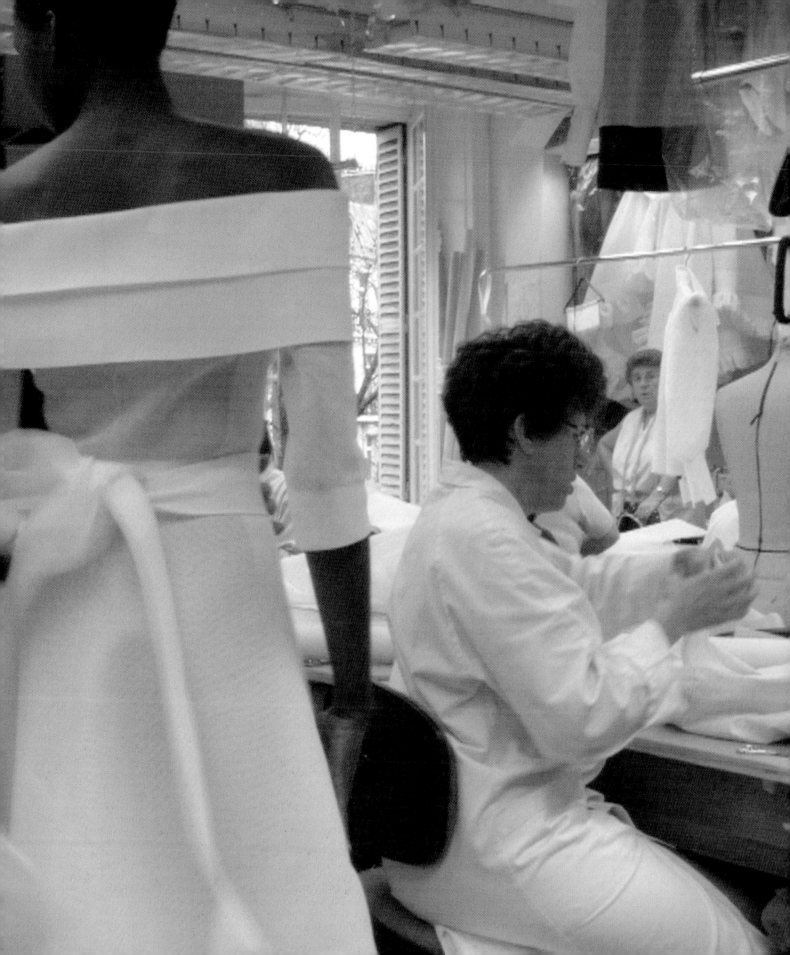

Once the pattern is made, the lines and volumes are examined again (they are rarely right the first time around) until the pattern is ready to be worn by a live model. It's only then, on a real woman, that Yves Saint Laurent can see how the piece works. Sometimes it lacks structure or doesn't express the idea in the sketch well enough, or sometimes he has to try to go in another direction. Yves Saint Laurent then asks that they start again. It's a real jump from wooden mannequin to model. The special few who witness this jump are the mirrors. They are indispensable, the truth comes from them—as long as they are seen with some objectivity. In haute couture, an eighth of an inch can make all the difference, and it is the master's eye that can catch this level of detail. When Saint Laurent is presented with a pattern on a model, he doesn't look at the woman, but at her reflection in the mirror. And when he finally has nothing more to say or change, he approves it. Now it's time to go from pattern to fabric choice.

ARRIVEE

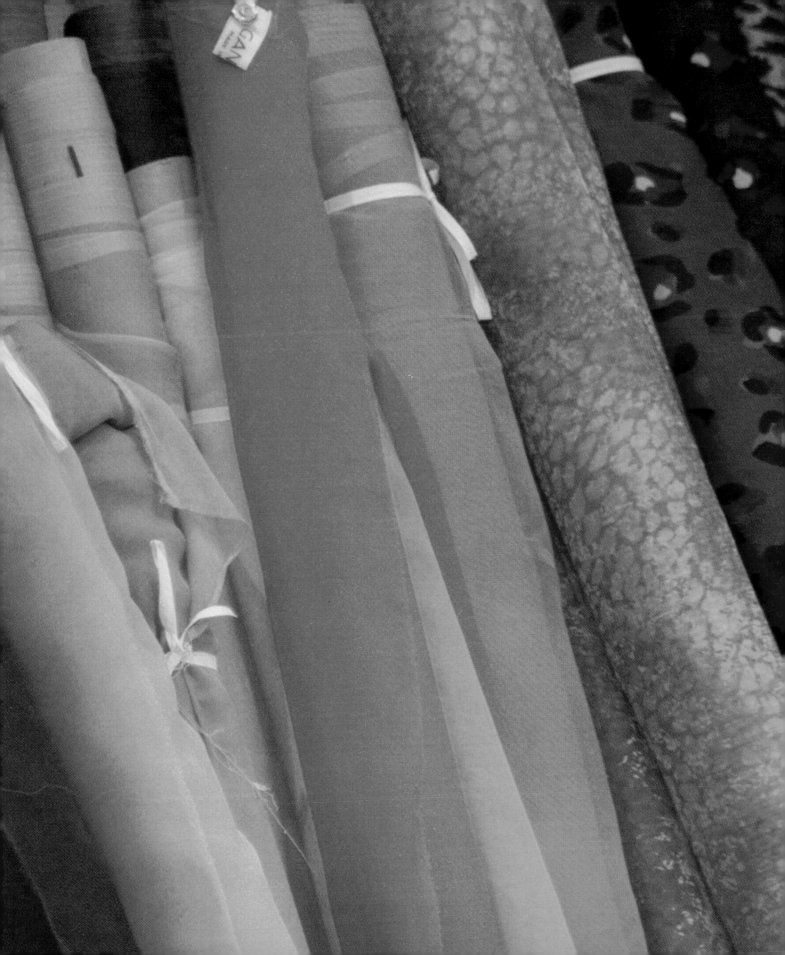

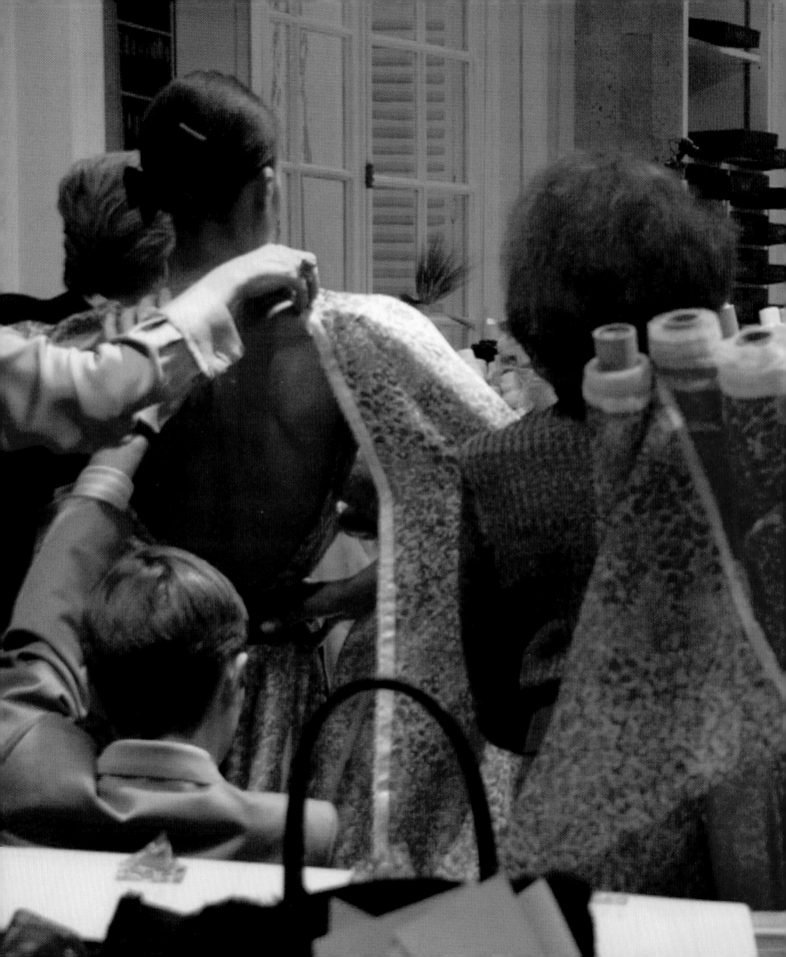

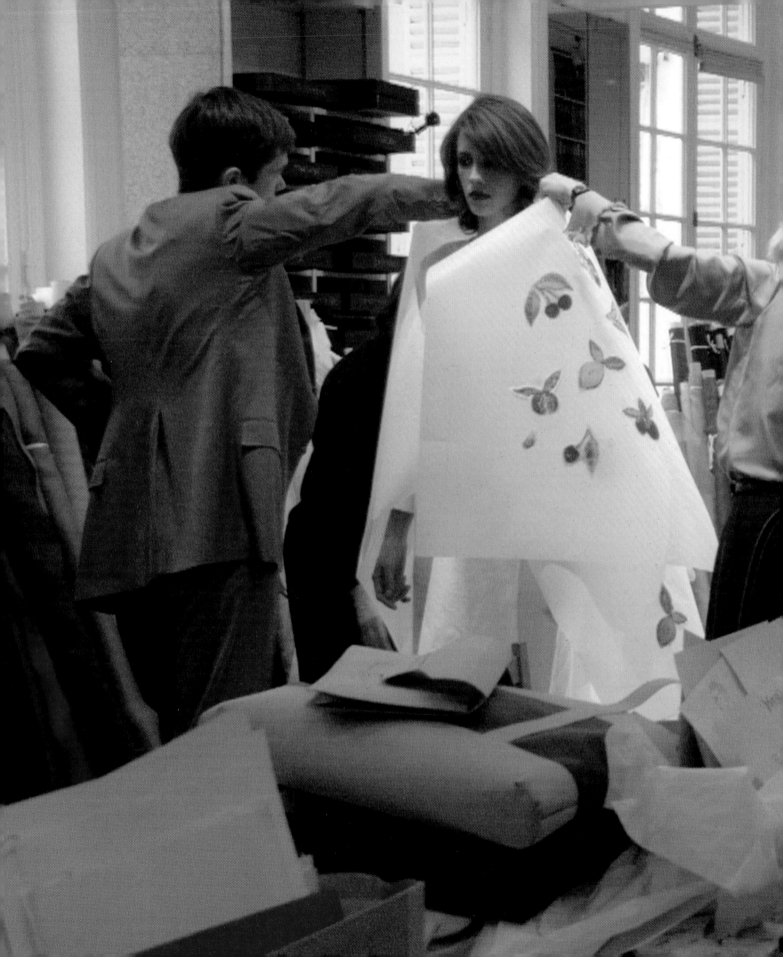

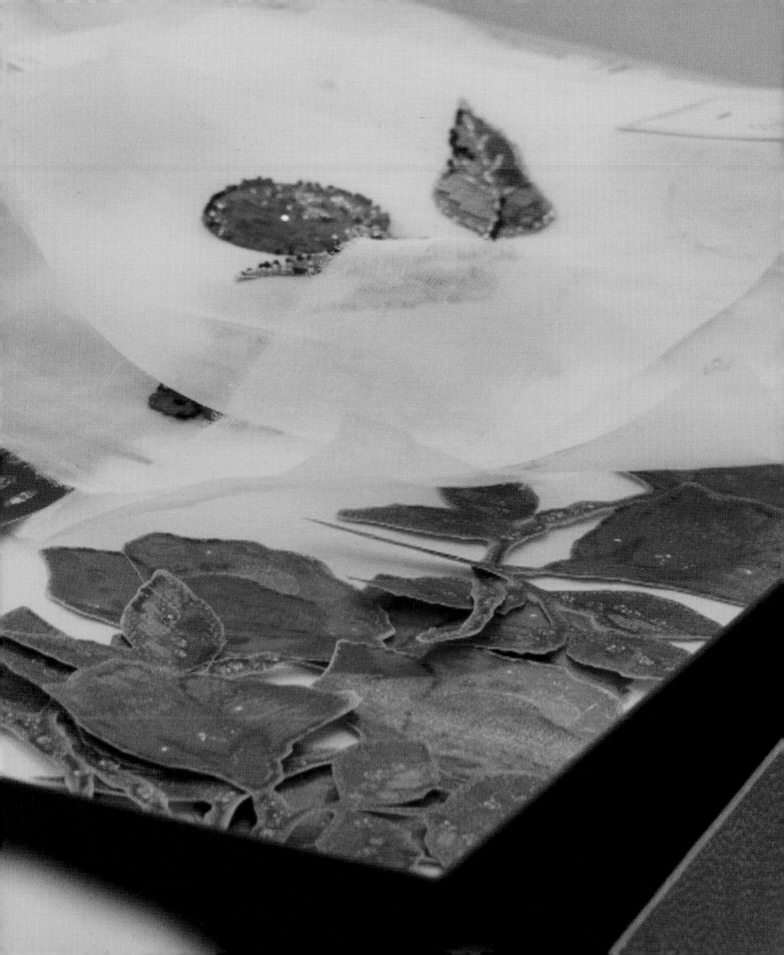

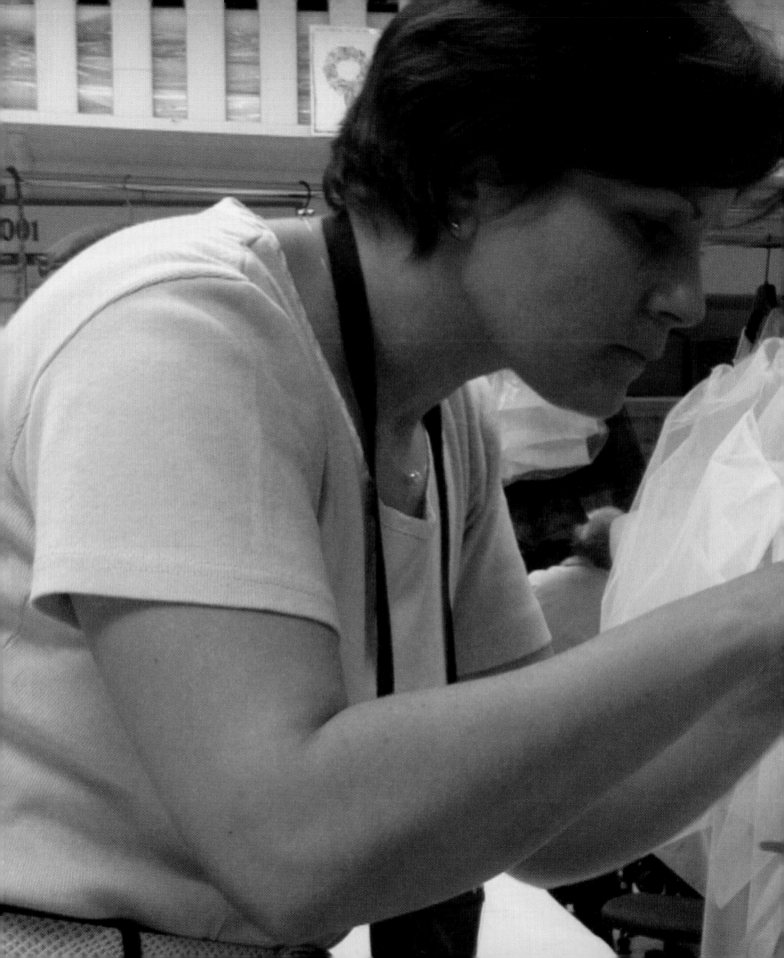

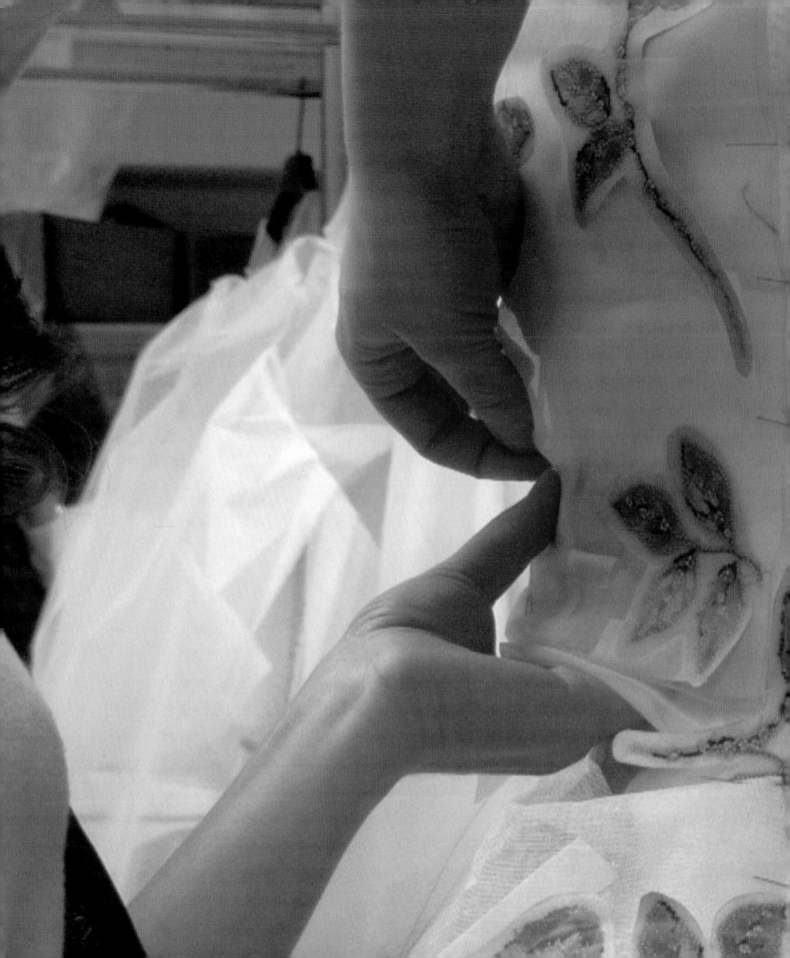

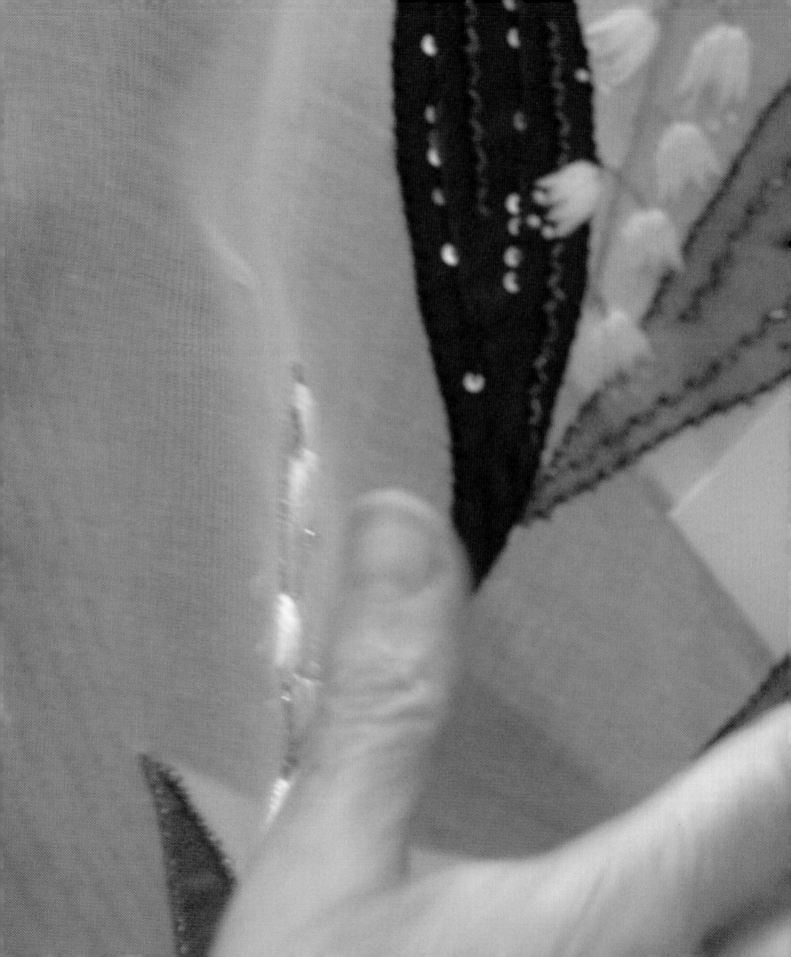

Le génie c'est l'Efance
retrouvée

Les modes passent le style est eternel.
La mode est futile le style pas

Il ne faut pas bruler
ses ailes aux feux de la
mode.

Le poison de la mode tue
Le style enrichit, develop
pe, fortifie.

Les femmes qui suivent de trop près
la mode courent un grand danger.
celui de perdre leur nature profonde,
leur style, leur elegance naturelle.

tout le monde peut s'amuser à créer
une mode. Peu de gens peuvent faire
un vrai vêtement.

la haute couture est une multitude
de secrets que l'on se chuchote. Rares
sont ceux qui ont le privilège de les
transmettre

Toute création n'est qu'une
~~En~~ re - création, une façon
nouvelle de voir les mêmes
choses, de les exprimer dif
feremment, de les préciser,
d'en exalter un angle
jusque là inaperçu ou
~~au contraire~~ d'en accuser
les contours.

Pour travailler et construire mes robes. il me faut un mannequin vivant. Un corps en mouvement Je ne pourrais pas travailler seulement sur un mannequin de Bois. Car pour moi ~~son~~ un vêtement doit vivre. et pour le mettre en scène ensuite dans la vie courante, il me faut ~~toujours~~ la presence d'un corps de femme.

Les mannequins trois ont le privilège ~~~~ d'avoir des proportions et des gestes particulièrement modernes. Ils s'adaptent parfaitement à ce que je veux et je dois dire qu'ils m'ont Toujours et régulièrement apporté J'aime la lumière qu'ils donnent aux tissus. Je pense que la

profondeur ~~de~~ de la cou
leur de leur peau fait ressortir
davantage l'Intensité des couleurs.

Ils ne m'ont jamais déçu, J'ai
me leur expression, leur démar
che, l'éclat de leurs yeux, leurs
lignes longues et ~~la~~ la
souplesse irresistible de leur
manière de Bouger.

Elles possèdent pour moi ce
qu'il y a de plus magique
chez une femme. Le Mystère.
~~mais~~ Pas ~~le mystère Fatal~~ le
vieux mystère des femmes fatales
mais le mystère dynamique
d'une femme d'Aujourd'hui

(sur le pantalon)

Depuis 1966 où le 1er
smoking a fait son appa
rution dans ma collection
l'idée d'une femme en
costume d'homme n'a
cessé de grandir, de s'appro
fondir, de s'imposer comme
la marque même d'une
femme d'aujourd'hui. Je
pense que s'il fallait re
présenter la femme des an
nées 70 un jour dans le
temps, c'est une femme
en pantalon qui s'imposerait
car à partir de 68 le pan
talon est devenu une des
pièces maitresse de la
garde robe d'une femme
moderne.

une femme en costume pan
talon est loin d'être mas
culine. A travers la coupe
implacable et rigoureuse
sa feminité, sa séduction
son ambiguité ressortent
davantage. Elle s'identi
fie au corps d'un adoles
cent c-a-d qu'elle
affirme le grand boulever
sement des moeurs qui

imanquablement tend
à l'uniformité et à
l'égalité des sexes.
Cette femme androgyne
égale à l'homme par son
vêtement bouleverse
l'image traditionnelle
d'une féminité ~~dépassé~~
classique et ~~triomphe~~
et dépassée et déploie
toutes les armes secrètes
et qui n'appartiennent l'age
qu'à elle (particulièrement le moven)
de ce qui semblerait être tu o m'plier et j'ai corrigé
un handicap, mais qui
n'est en réalité que
l'image mystérieuse et
séduisante ~~dans~~ de la
femme d'aujourd'hui

à mettre en parallèle
avec l'affirmation du
pantalon, du costume
pantalon et du blazer
(~~triomphe~~) l'énorme phéno
mène du jean chez les
jeunes femmes

Mon enfance ne veut pas
mourir. Elle se prolonge
en moi ainsi qu'un secret

Toute œuvre est bonne dans
la mesure où elle exprime
l'Homme qui l'a créée

~~XXXX~~

Il y a les tricheurs qui
utilisent une puissance
dont la source est hors
d'eux

BONNARD

ERN   MARILYN MONROE   SCH

Dahl-Wolfe

HARAJAS' JEWELS

Going from the pattern to the fabric is a delicate matter. The vendors who have worked with him know Yves Saint Laurent's preferred palettes. They send him swatches of fabric that are then laid out before him. Beneath the vigilant gaze of his collaborators, Anne-Marie Muñoz and Loulou de la Falaise, he selects the cloth that is most suited to the article of clothing. He likes his suits to be constructed of dry-spun fabrics that most resemble the first pencil stroke. His favorite color is black, which is most evocative of his sketches. Often, it is men's fabrics that suggest themselves. He gathers them up with both hands and arranges them over the model's body. He stands back, assesses the effect—and then decides. For "softness" (dresses), the fabrics begin in brighter colors—even if they end up being black and navy blue. Yves Saint Laurent is a couturier who takes on the challenge of color. His rigor requires of him the kind of clean cut without which no extravagance is possible.

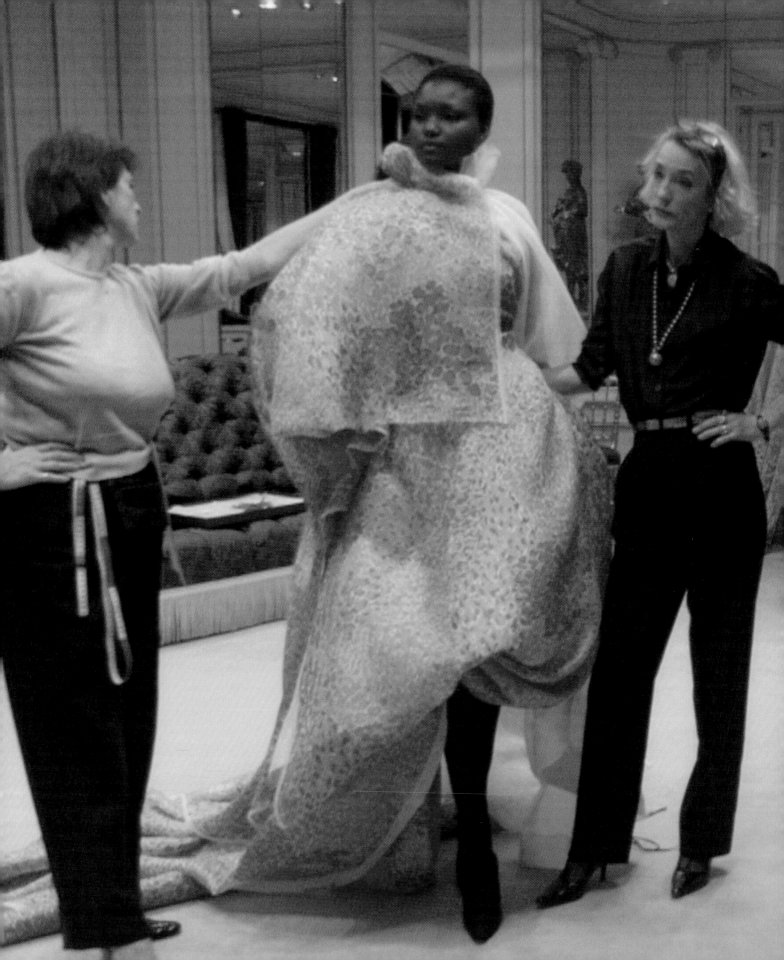

MOD

Confini (signature)

Atelier

Mannequin

Nom du modèle

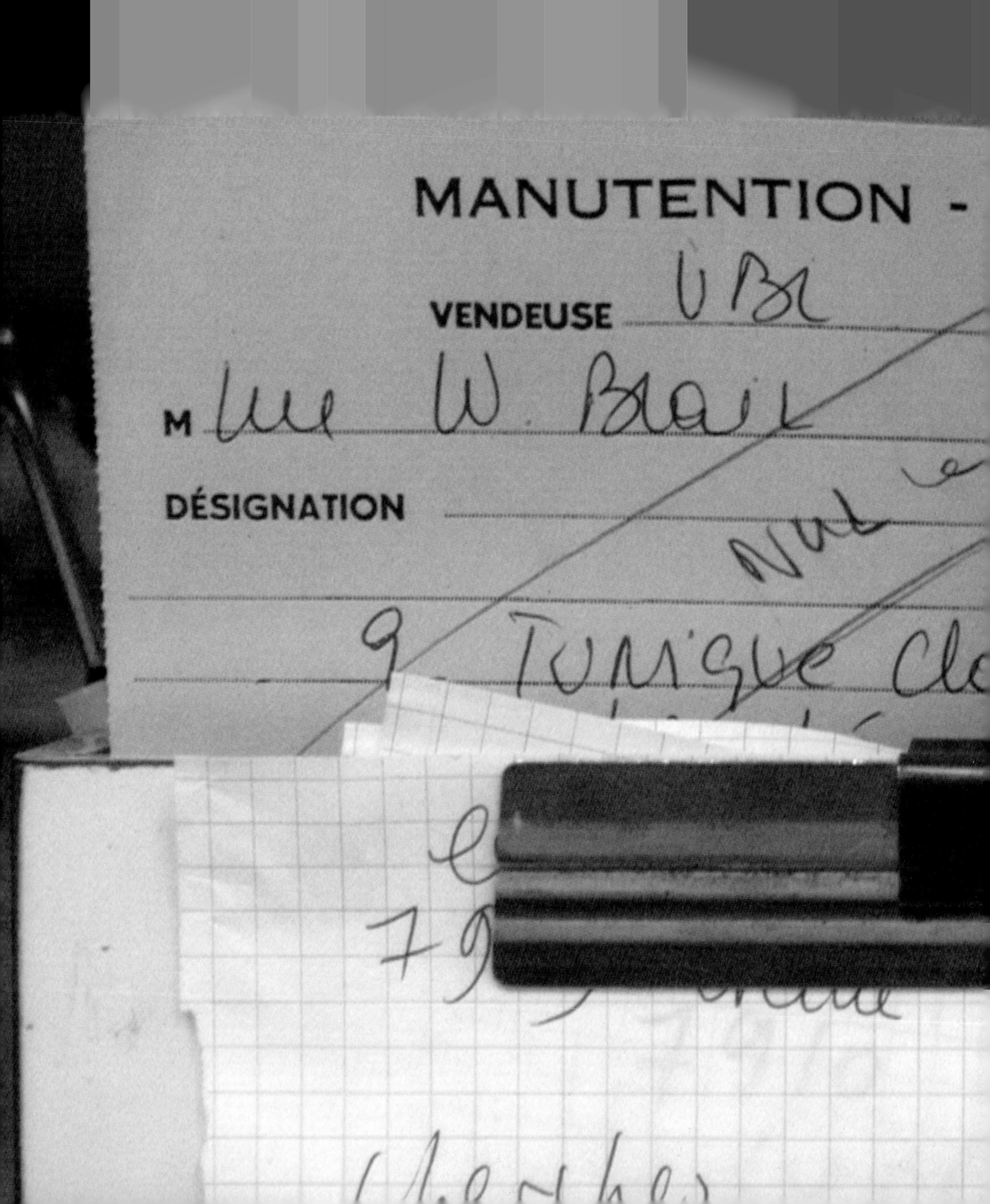

MANUTENTION -

VENDEUSE UBL

M Mme W. Blai

DÉSIGNATION

Nel e

9 Tunique Cl

ɪᴇʀ *Colette*

17 17 19 1000 № 072379

7 7

le 9
vert 7
re 0

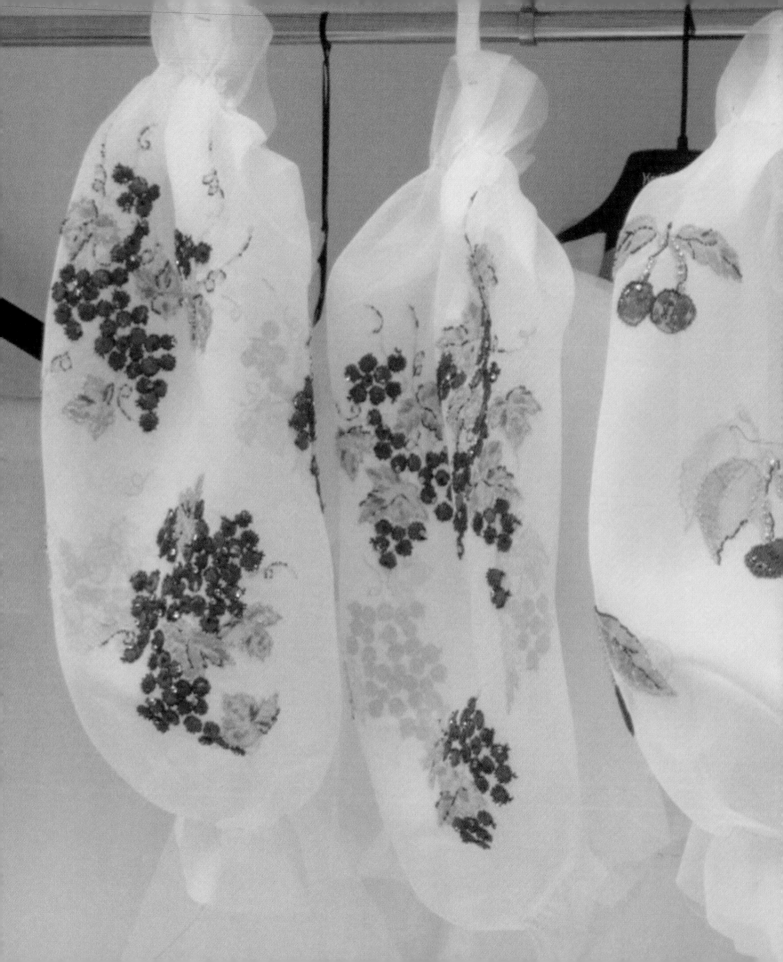

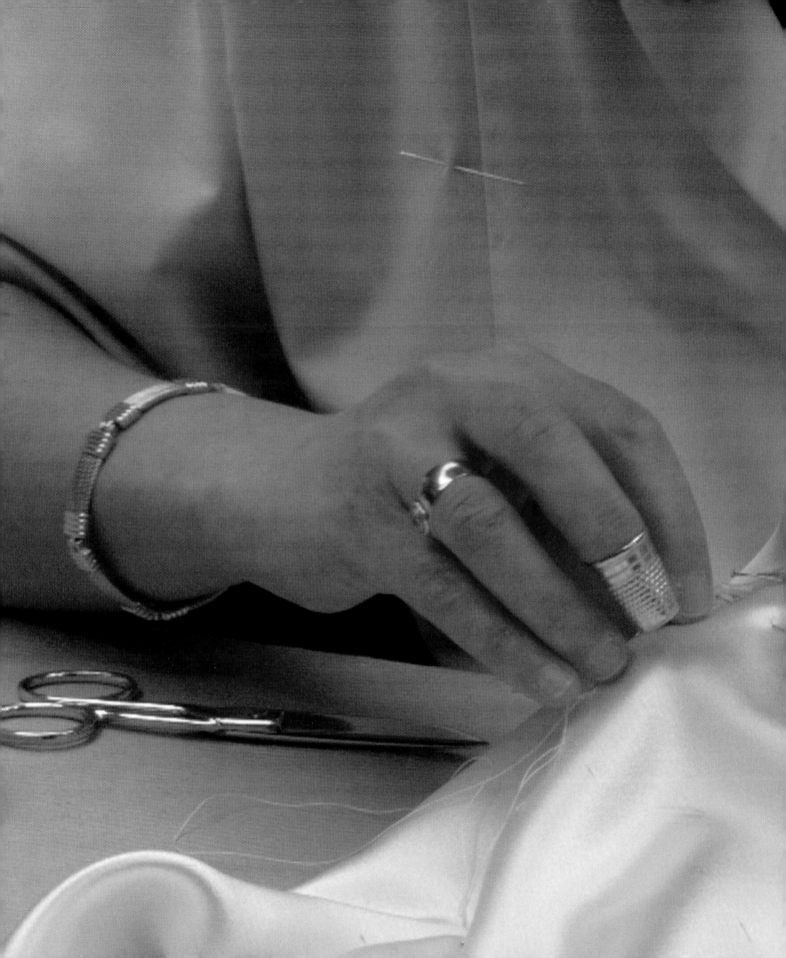

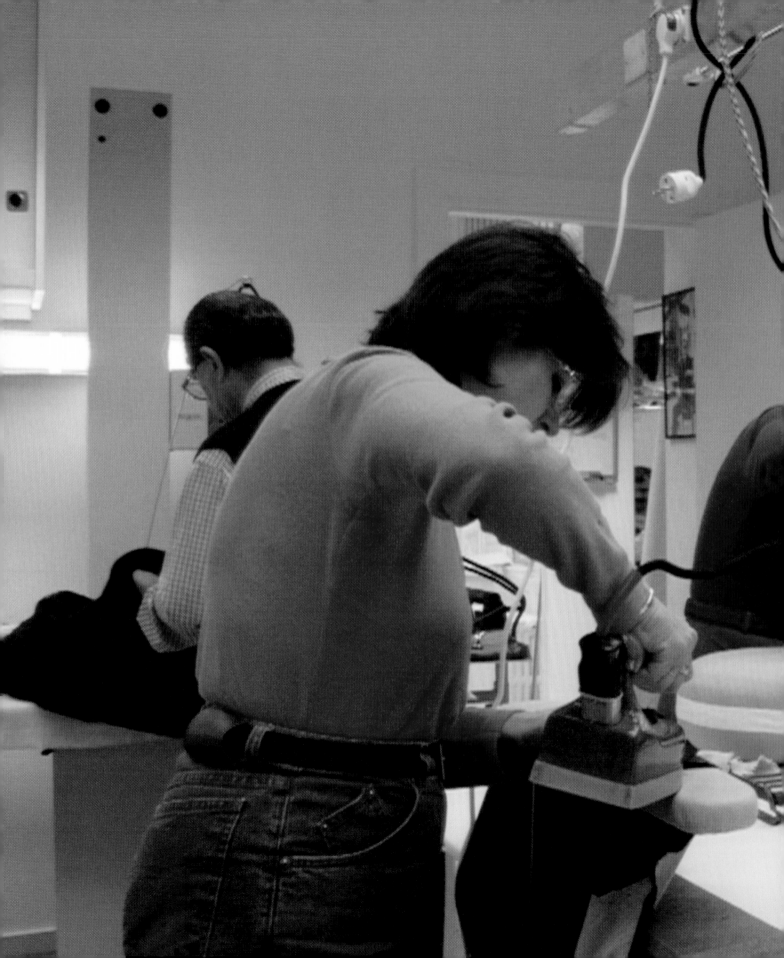

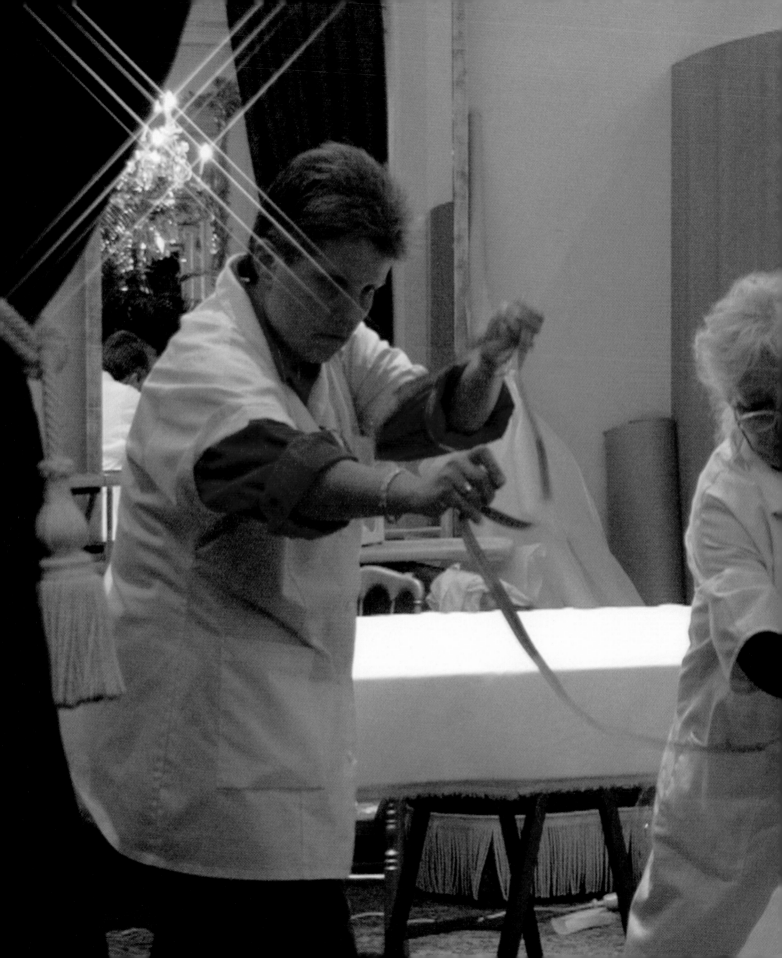

ARRIVEE

ARRIVEE

The runway show will take place in a few days. Yves Saint Laurent leaves his atelier for the Grand Salon. Before the designer gives his final approval, last adjustments are made to the clothes, presented by the models who will wear them in the show. Accompanied by his longtime collaborator, Anne-Marie Muñoz, whom he met at Dior in 1955, and by Loulou de la Falaise, director of the accessories department, Yves Saint Laurent looks his creations over one last time. Under the designer's attentive eye, Loulou accessorizes the models with jewels, hats, and gloves. As if to emphasize the finality of the moment, the makeup man, the hairdresser, and all the atelier's workers congregate. Before they appear on the runway, the designs will live their "lives" far from the haute couture house and the gaze of their creator.

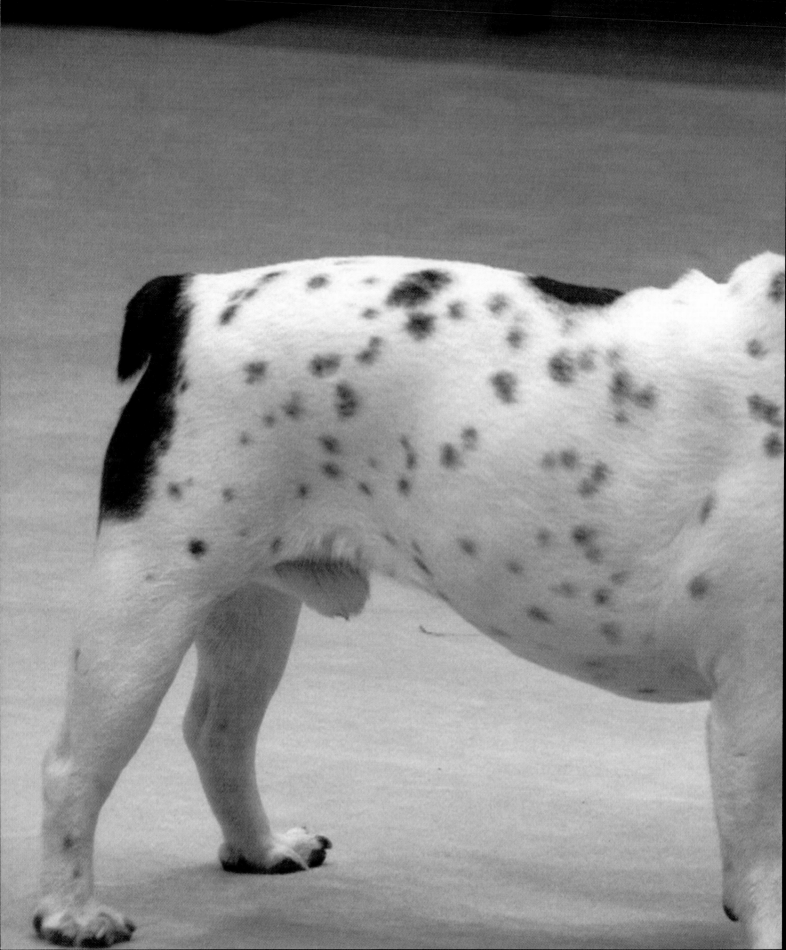

La lumière qui emane d'un
être qui aime est incomparable

Seul l'Amour preserve la beauté d'un
être.
L'amour est le meilleur remède au
vieillissement

L'amour vous donne des
ailes que la vie se
charge de couper

Les plus belles victoires
sont celles que l'on fait
sur soi même.

Il faut tout faire pour
eviter le Regret.

Rien n'est plus beau qu'un
corps nu
Le plus beau vêtement qui
puisse habiller une femme
ce sont les bras de l'homme qu'elle aime.
Mais pour celles qui n'ont
pas eu la chance de trouver
ce bonheur ~~je~~ Je suis là.

la mode est une fête
s'habiller c'est ~~une~~
se préparer à jouer
un role.
une femme ne devient
emouvante qu'à partir
du moment où elle triche
et où l'Artifice commence
à jouer.
je ne suis pas un couturier
je suis un artisan.
un fabricant de bonheur

chaque 25 ans le corps change
les gestes les attitudes changent
There is a new body emerging
slim and long is
and this body est more
important than any revolution
dictated pour by any designer.

The drama for luxury is that
there are so many stupid
rich people. Luxury so few
Know how to use it and
make it respectable,

Quand on se sent bien dans
un vêtement tout peut arriver
~~C'est un passeport~~
~~Quand~~ Un bon vêtement c'est
un passeport pour le bonheur

Parler de ⎯⎯⎯
Revolution dans la mode est
~~un mot~~ perimé.
la veritable Revolution est
ailleurs. C'est celle de
l'esprit. ~~celle~~ qui dictera
celle de la mode.

La jeunesse

Vieillir c'est commencer à
penser aux autres.
La jeunesse est égoïste.

La jeunesse est une
maladie dont on guérit
souvent très tard. Cer-
tains même n'y parvien-
nent pas et en meurent.

L'inquiétude de vieillir
vient de ne pas s'être
trouvé.

On peut avoir honte de son bonheur. Jamais de sa souffrance.

La joie et le bonheur peuvent ~~être~~ ~~sont~~ des mirages qui nous cachent la réalité des choses et des êtres

La sérénité est la jeunesse des vieillards. C'est sûrement aussi beau que la jeunesse. C'est un luxe à la portée de tous, l'aboutissement d'une vie et sa consécration. C'est le contraire d'1 privilège.

La seule morale possible d'un bout à l'autre de l'existence de l'homme est l'Art. A travers lui il peut espérer approcher le Bonheur.

Je pense qu'il n'y a sur terre qu'un seul bonheur possible. Celui de s'oublier et de se consacrer aux autres. En essayant de faire le bonheur des autres, on finit par en recevoir quelques éclats.

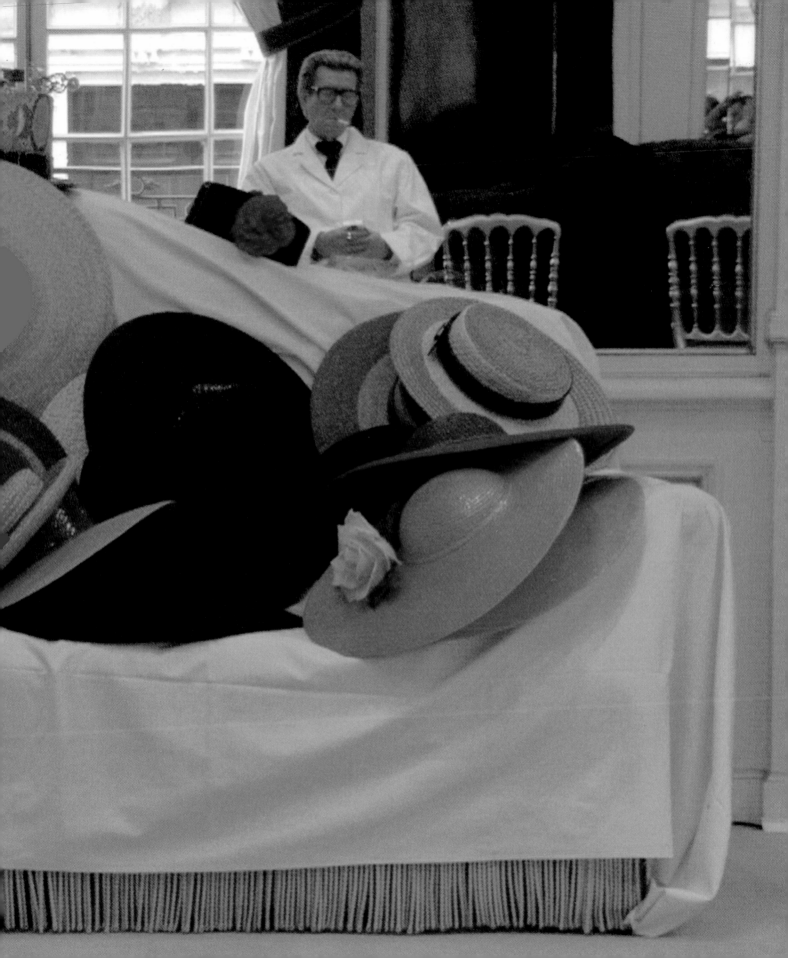

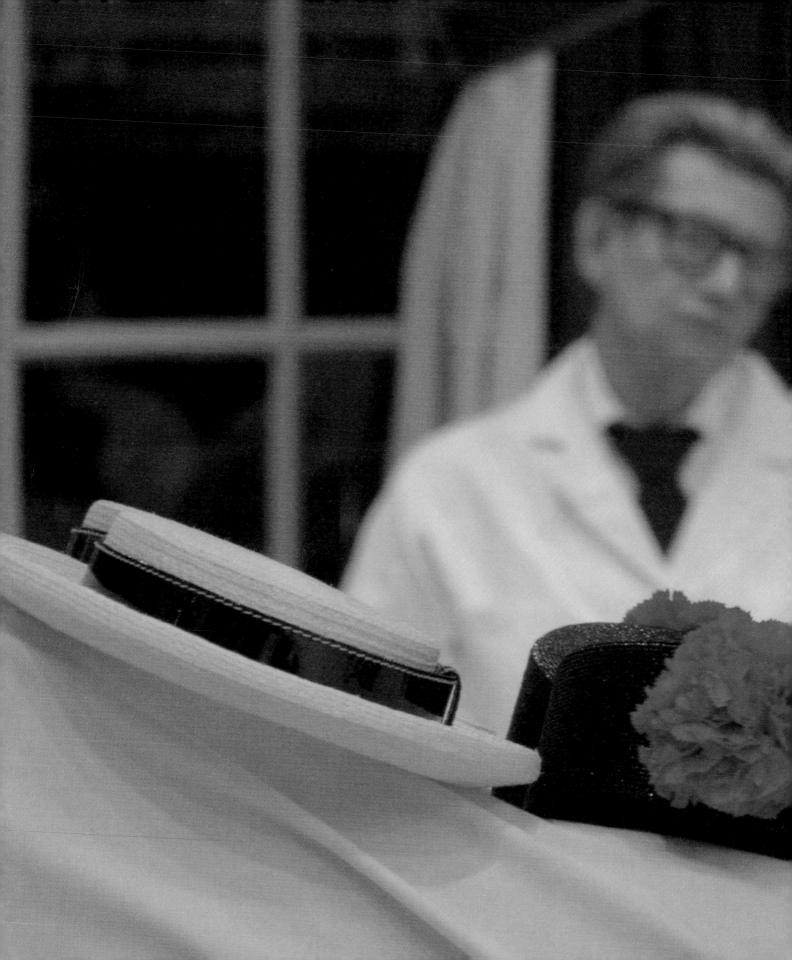

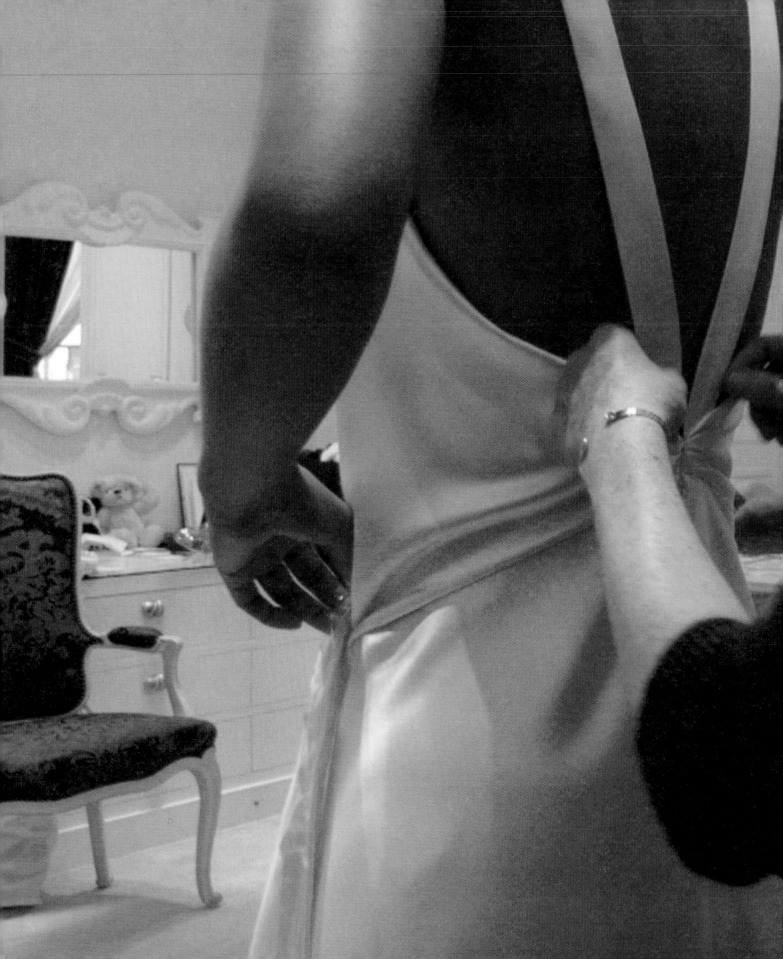

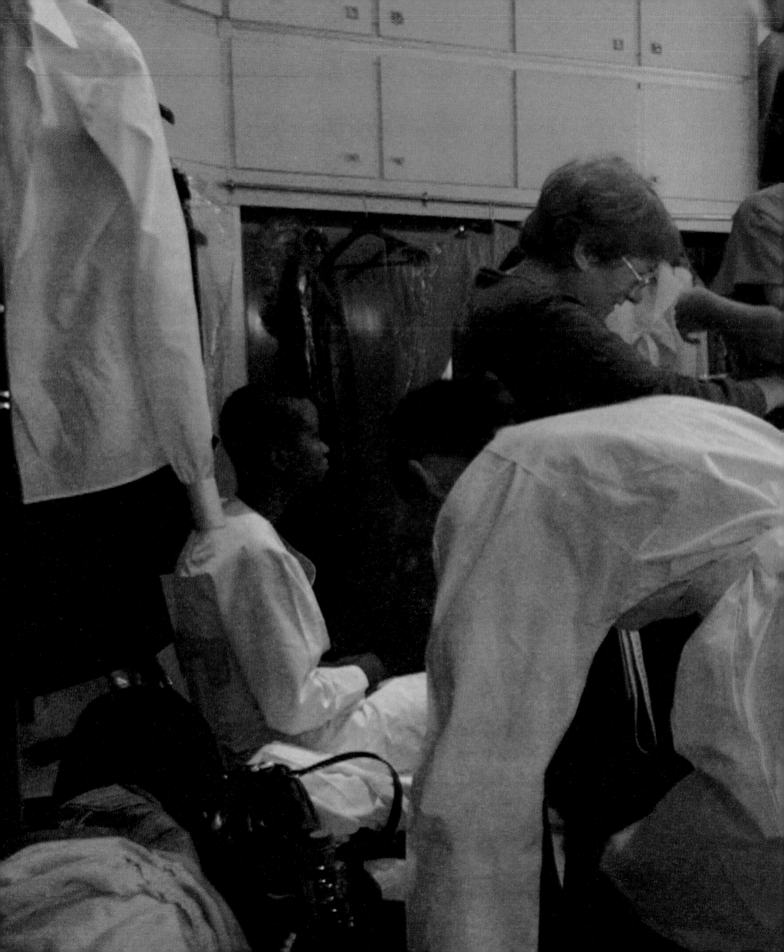

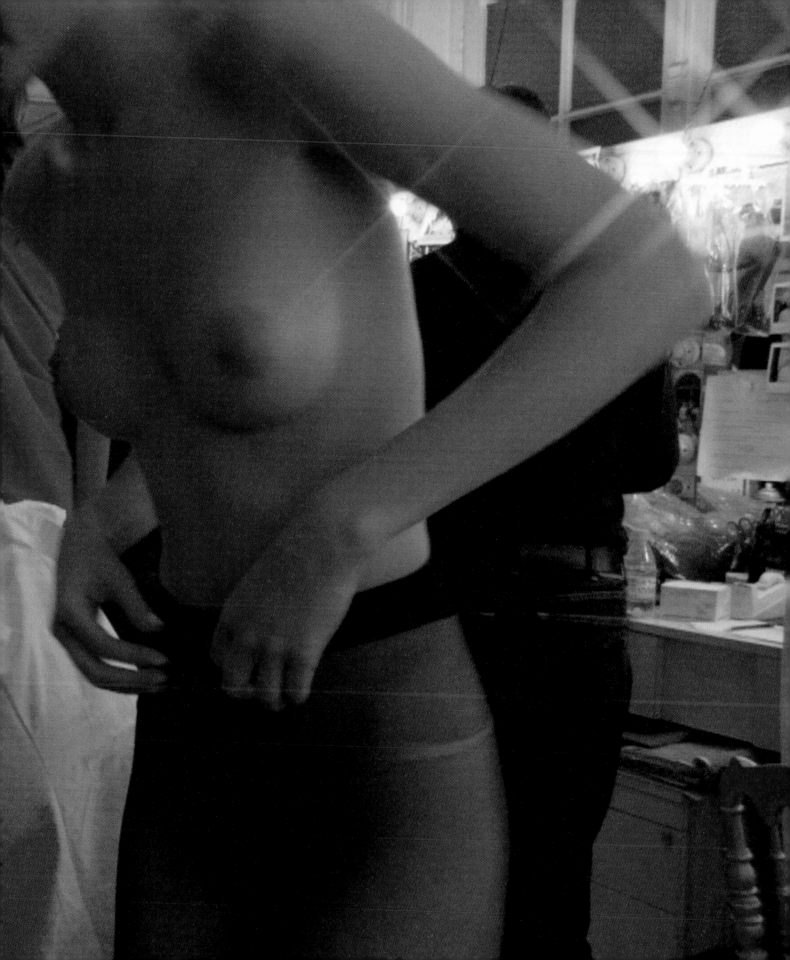

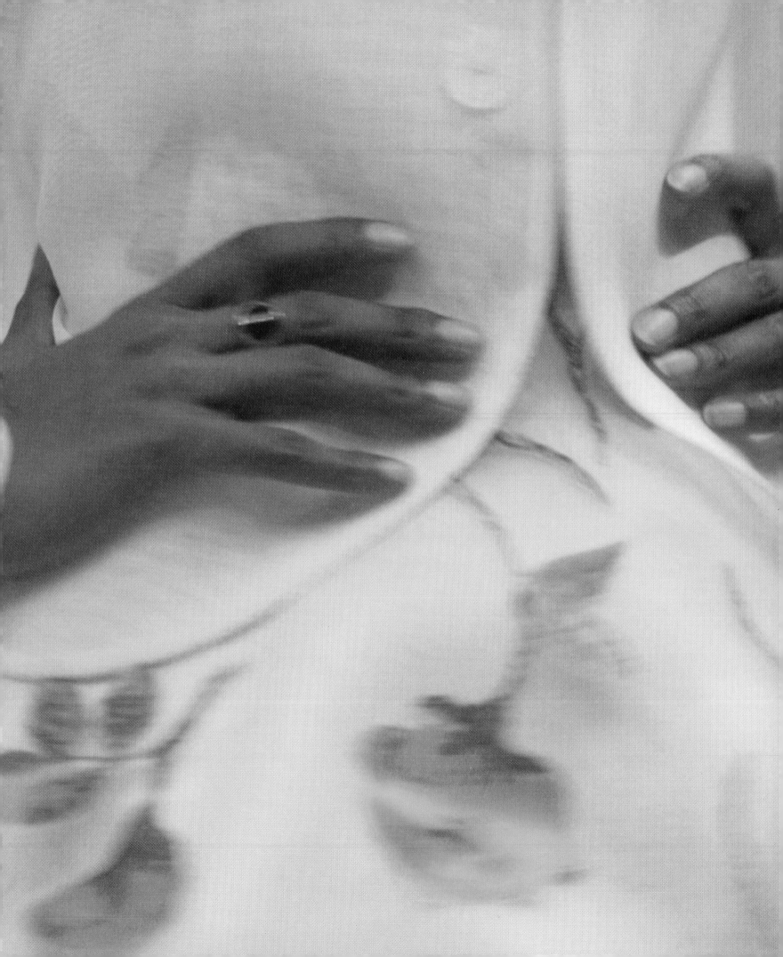

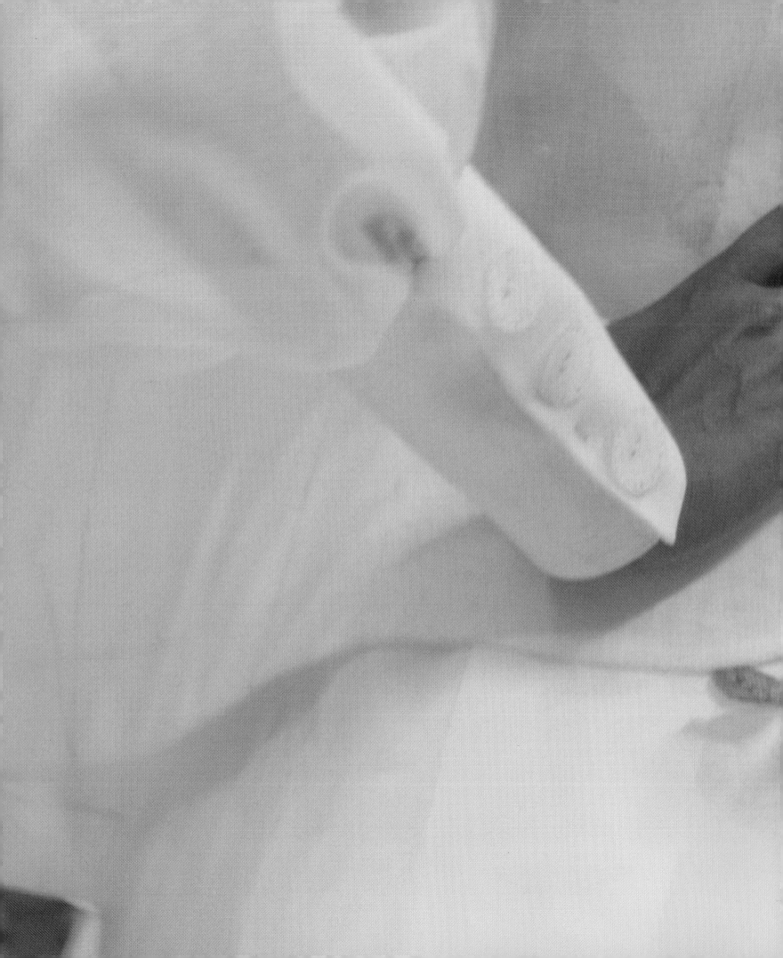

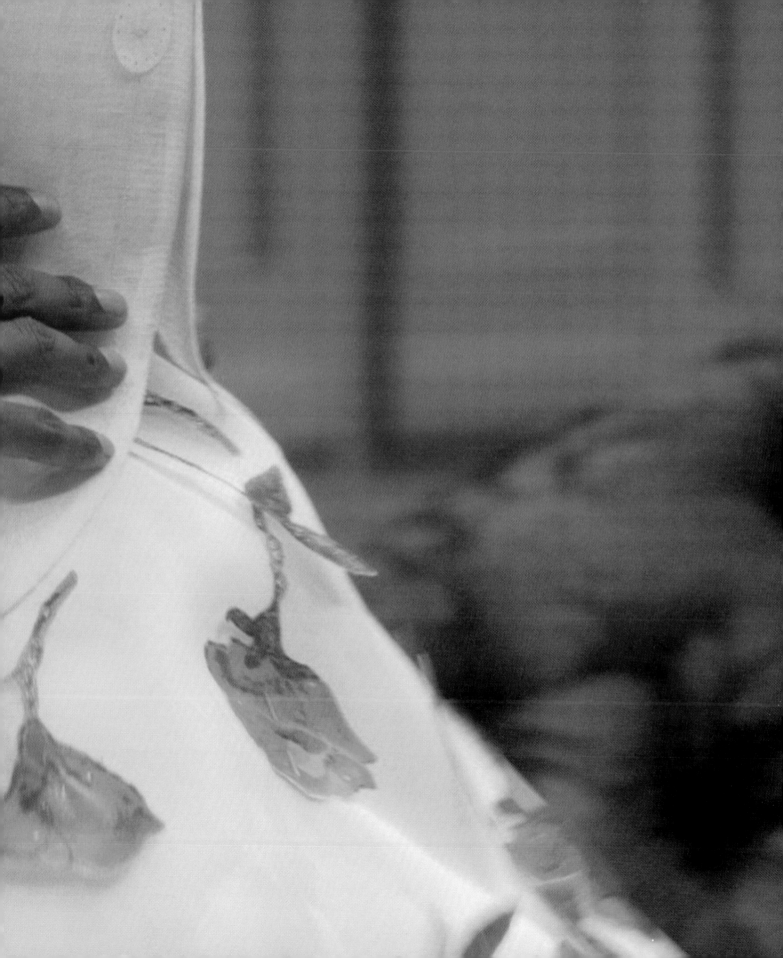

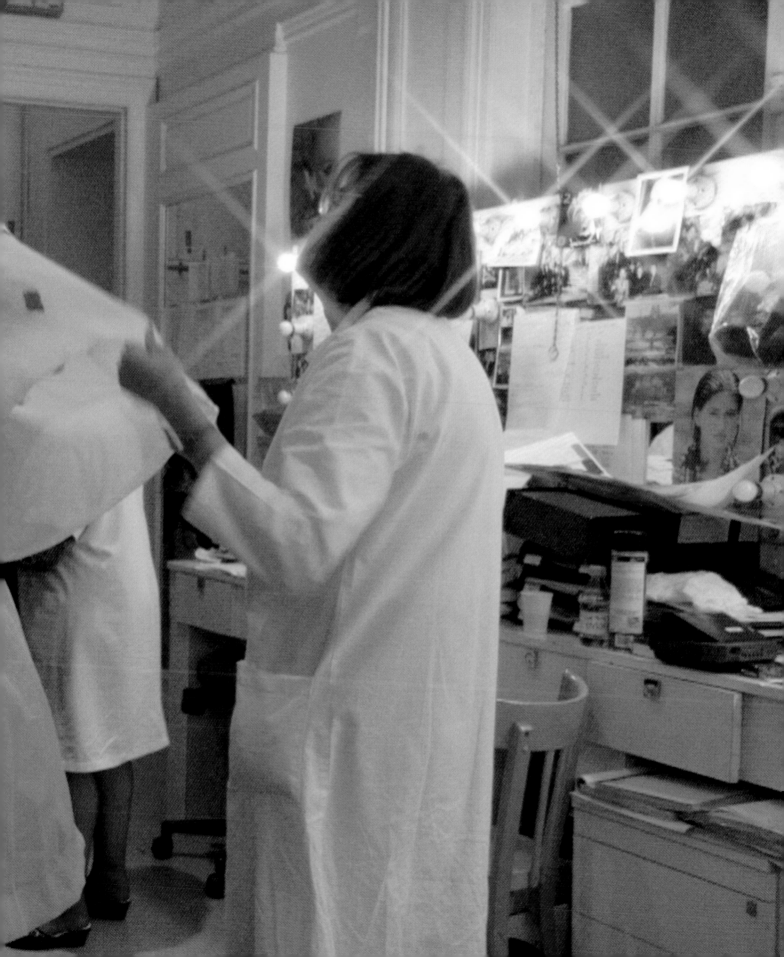

L'elegance c'est une façon de se mouvoir. C'est aussi savoir s'adapter à toutes les circons- tances de sa vie.
Sans elegance de Coeur, il n'y a pas d'elegance

Yves Saint Laurent

0 8. JAN. 1986

N1:   N2:   ID:

JE SUIS COMME ON DIT UN ''HOMME A CHIEN''. C'EST A DIRE QUE JE VIS
COMPLETEMENT AVEC LUI. LA NUIT ET LE JOUR. EN VOYAGE, JE L'EMMENE ET
LORSQUE C'EST IMPOSSIBLE, COMME EN ANGLETERRE PAR EXEMPLE, JE RESTE
CHEZ MOI. IL A ETE BAPTISE MOUJIK PAR LILI BRIK QUI VECUT AVEC
MAIAKOVSKI ET QUI EUT SUR LE POETE RUSSE UNE INFLUENCE CONSIDERABLE.
DEPUIS, LILI EST MORTE MAIS MOUJIK EST LA, BIEN VIVANT. NOUS AVONS
NOS HABITUDES TOUS LES DEUX, NOS MANIES. JE CROIS SURTOUT QUE NOUS
AVONS LES MEMES GOUTS. C'EST IMPORTANT. IL Y A DES TISSUS QU'IL AIME
-NE RIEZ PAS- LE BRUIT DU TAFFETAS QU'ON DEROULE LE REND FOU. IL A
MEME DEFILE DANS UNE COLLECTION: IL ACCOMPAGNAIT UN TAILLEUR NOIR ET
BLANC COMME LUI.
AUSSI, LORSQUE MON AMI PIERRE BERGE M'A OFFERT POUR LE DERNIER NOEL
SON PORTRAIT PAR ANDY WARHOL, J'AI ETE SUBMERGE DE JOIE ET D'EMOTION.
C'ETAIT MOUJIK, MAIS C'ETAIT AUSSI ANDY QUI AVAIT PEINT MON PROPRE
PORTRAIT IL Y A PLUS DE QUINZE ANS. DEPUIS, ANDY ET MOI NOUS NE NOUS
VOYONS PAS SOUVENT MAIS JE SAIS TOUT DE LUI, DE SA CARRIERE, DE SON
OEUVRE ET MON ADMIRATION POUR LUI N'A JAMAIS FAILLI. ALORS, N'HESI-
TONS PAS ET DISONS LE SANS DETOUR: MOUJIK PAR ANDY C'EST LE PLUS BEAU
CADEAU DE NOEL QUE JE POUVAIS ESPERER.

                          YVES SAINT LAURENT

"La sagesse est d'être, à certains moments, fou" (Cocteau). Ma fantaisie peut être tendre, raffinée, poétique ou barbare, sauvage. Rompant avec toutes les règles, je saisis alors l'âme de la rue, des évènements de tous les jours. Je transmets mes fantasmes, je les adapte à mon métier, je les rends accessibles avant tout au corps d'une femme.

Parfois, il y a un grand combat en moi entre ces fantasmes et ce corps de femme dont la règle est que je le respecte. C'est toujours le corps de la Femme qui triomphe, qui gagne et je m'efface derrière elle afin de ne pas trahir la vérité de mon métier, ma vérité profonde qui est l'humilité de mes idées devant la réalité d'un corps de femme.

La seduction : s'aimer un peu pour plaire beaucoup.

Le plus beau maquillage pour une femme est une passion.

C'est à l'heure où sa jeunesse commence à s'estomper qu'une femme devient de plus en plus emouvante.

La vie n'est possible que grâce à
des fantômes esthétiques.

————————

La mode est une ~~chose~~ maladie ~~irrésistible~~ Incurable
~~constante~~ Le grand art, à dit
Metternich, est de durer

Toute ma vie je me souviendrai de mon adolescence et de ~~mon~~ ma jeunesse passées dans ce merveilleux pays qu'était l'Algérie Je ne me sens pas pieds noirs. Je me sens Francais d'Algérie.
Mes souvenirs me ramènent si fortement aux jours merveilleux de ce qu'était Oran où je suis né. Je revois cette belle ville avec son melange de races.

Algériens, Français, Italiens, Espagnols qui imprimaient leurs bonne humeur, leur gaîté leur folie de vivre passionnement ma famille dont les origines sont alsaciennes ~~et~~ avait débarqué sur ce sol alors aride en 1870 pour ne pas être sous l'occupasion allemande. Le même exode en sens contraire allait se produire ~~ont~~ en 1962 ayant tout perdu.

Un corps de Femme Nue que je dois
habiller sans ~~toute~~ porter atteinte
à la liberté de ~~ses~~ mouvements
naturels. Bref, mon métier
et le dialogue amoureux de
cette femme nue ~~⬚~~ avec tous
les sortilèges des enroulements de
Tissus

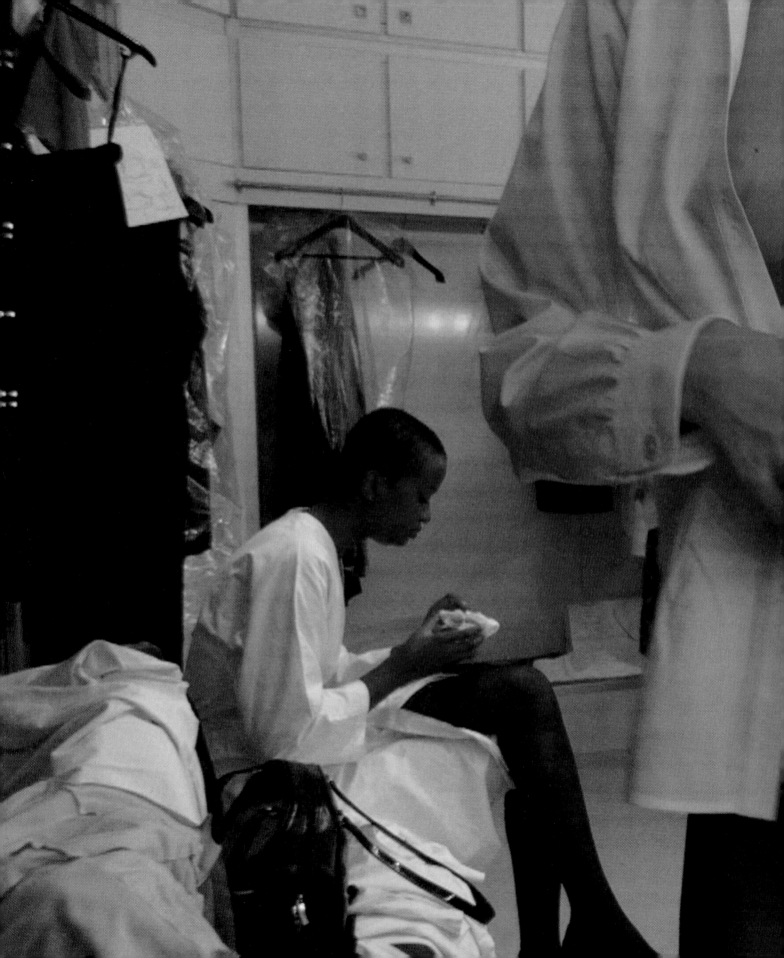

ARRIVEE

Hotel Intercontinental, Salon Impérial, Paris, Wednesday January 24th 2001, 12:30 pm

Collections 1962 – 2002

1962, Spring - Summer, *Collection Cabans et Marinières*
1962, Fall - Winter, *Collection Robin des Bois et Blouse de Normand*
1963, Spring - Summer, *Collection Robes Marines à Cols Blancs*
1963, Fall - Winter, *Collection Vareuses et Cuissardes*
1964, Spring - Summer, *Collection Jupes Paysannes*
1964, Fall - Winter, *Collection Dentelles*
1965, Spring - Summer
1965, Fall - Winter, *Collection Mondrian Poliakoff et Mariée de Tricot*
1966, Spring - Summer, *Collection Marins et Casquettes*
1966, Fall - Winter, *Collection Pop Art - 1er Smoking*
1967, Spring - Summer, *Collection Africaine*
1967, Fall - Winter, *Collection Reine Christine et Robes Plissées*
1968, Spring - Summer, *Collection Saharienne et Smoking Short*
1968, Fall - Winter, *Collection Transparence et Jumpsuit*
1969, Spring - Summer, *Collection Patchwork Robes Perlées et Tailleur Pantalon Saharienne*
1969, Fall - Winter, *Collection Robes Sculptures Lalanne*
1970, Spring - Summer, *Collection Mini Panthère et Tailleur Pantalon*
1970, Fall - Winter, *Collection Manteaux Patchwork*
1971, Spring - Summer, *Collection 40*
1971, Fall - Winter, *Collection Bal Proust*
1972, Spring - Summer
1972, Fall - Winter, *Collection Cardigans Brodés*
1973, Spring - Summer, *Collection Les Pyjamas*
1973, Fall - Winter, *Collection Cardigans de Tricot et Kilts*
1974, Spring - Summer, *Collection Prince de Galles et Robes Chemisiers*
1974, Fall - Winter, *Collection Robes de Bal et Robes Noires*
1975, Spring - Summer, *Collection Look Sirene*
1975, Fall - Winter, *Collection Panne et Mousseline*
1976, Spring - Summer, *Collection Tailleurs Pantalons Blancs*
1976, Fall - Winter, *Collection Opéra Ballets Russes*
1977, Spring - Summer, *Collection Les Espagnoles et Les Romantiques*
1977, Fall - Winter, *Collection Les Chinoises Opium*
1978, Spring - Summer, *Collection Broadway Suit*
1978, Fall - Winter, *Collection Pure Elégance*
1979, Spring - Summer, *Collection Les Classiques Saint Laurent*
1979, Fall - Winter, *Collection Hommage à Picasso et Diaghilev*
1980, Spring - Summer, *Collection Delightful Dress Courses*
1980, Fall - Winter, *Collection Shakespeare Look Hommage à Cocteau - Aragon - Appolinaire*
1981, Spring - Summer, *Collection Les Impressionnistes*
1981, Fall - Winter, *Collection Matisse et Bubble Dress*
1982, Spring - Summer, *Collection Clean and Sophisticated et l'Inde*
1982, Fall - Winter, *Collection The Fit Revolution*
1983, Spring - Summer, *Collection Dress Right*
1983, Fall - Winter, *Collection Paris*

1984, Spring - Summer, *Collection Les Grands Classiques*

1984, Fall - Winter, *Collection Yves Saint Laurent Super Women*

1985, Spring - Summer, *Collection African Queen*

1985, Fall - Winter, *Collection Spare Chic*

1986, Spring - Summer, *Collection Tender Chic*

1986, Fall - Winter, *Collection Féminine Glamour et Les Panthères*

1987, Spring - Summer, *Collection Hommage à David Hockney*

1987, Fall - Winter, *Collection Les Plumes*

1988, Spring - Summer, *Collection Cubiste Hommage à Braque*

1988, Fall - Winter, *Collection Les Raisins de la Colère*

1989, Spring - Summer, *Collection Modern and Sexy*

1989, Fall - Winter, *Collection Les Brocarts*

1990, Spring - Summer, *Collection Les Hommages*

1990, Fall - Winter, *Collection Les Félines et Les Tailleurs Lainage et Dentelle*

1991, Spring - Summer, *Collection Les Robes à Capuche*

1991, Fall - Winter, *Collection Les Robes Guêpières*

1992, Spring - Summer, *Collection Inspiration Matisse au Maroc*

1992, Fall - Winter, *Collection Tailleur Redingote et Brassières*

1993, Spring - Summer, *Collection Les Fleurs de Giverny*

1993, Fall - Winter, *Collection Les Minis*

1994, Spring - Summer, *Collection Les Tailleurs Pantalons et Les 4 Watteau*

1994, Fall - Winter, *Collection Les Manteaux Mandarins*

1995, Spring - Summer, *Collection Les Papillons*

1995, Fall - Winter, *Collection Les Robes Infantes et Les Tailleurs Chinois*

1996, Spring - Summer, *Collection Les Années 40 et Les Robes Lingerie*

1996, Fall - Winter, *Collection Tuniques de Jersey et Dentelle brodée*

1997, Spring - Summer, *Collection Opposite Attract Tout le monde dit " I love you "*

1997, Fall - Winter, *Collection Luxe Renaissance*

1998, Spring - Summer, *Collection Chic Rules*

1998, Fall - Winter, *Collection Black and White Elegance*

1999, Spring - Summer, *Collection The Nude Look*

1999, Fall - Winter, *Collection Les Blouses à la Roumaine*

2000, Spring - Summer, *Collection Le Jour en Saharienne Le Soir en Gitane*

2000, Fall - Winter, *Collection Tout Terriblement*

2001, Spring - Summer, *Collection Paris (les broderies)*

2001, Fall - Winter, *Collection La Renaissance*

2002, Spring - Summer, *Quarante ans de La Maison Yves Saint Laurent*

post-synchronisation
Pierre Hanau
timing
Caroline Champetier
conforming
Stéphane Longepierre

technical direction & distribution
Jean-Christophe Coin
Serge Bunel
Serge Martin
Hervé Collenot

postproduction
Ludovic de Maistre

production assistants
Iana Dontcheva
Natacha Gomes de Almeida
Katherine Prewitt
Pierre Geismar
Benoît Thibaut

production director
Olivier Gallais

production administrator
Stéphanie Combot
Janick Favret
Renzo d'Orlando

a coproduction

MOVIMENTO PRODUCTION
Christian Baute & Dominique Andreani

CANAL +
Documentary department
Anna Glogowski

CANAL+

TRANSATLANTIC VIDEO
Pierre de Rohan Chabot

in association with
Westdeutscher Rundfunk Köln
Werner Dütsch

with the participation of
The Centre National de la Cinématographie
du Ministère des affaires étrangères
and TV5

with the support of
the PROCIREP
PRODUCTION

At age fourteen, Yves Saint Laurent declared to whomever would listen that his name would shine one day "in golden letters on the Champs-Elysées." Soon after, he pictured himself a couturier in the Place Vendôme, where he imagined he was the designer of an haute couture collection with clothes that he would name and at prices that he would carefully set. These dreams weren't entirely fantasy—nor illusion. For by the time he was a teenager, his first fashion designs were attracting the attention of Michel de Brunhoff, the director of French *Vogue*, who decided to become his mentor and to introduce him to Christian Dior. Saint Laurent was not even eighteen when he won the Wool Secretariat prize. This is when the press discovered him. He earned great recognition for the first time when he was twenty-one years old, when he signed his first haute couture collection for Christian Dior. At this point, he reached a peak from which he would never fall. In Algeria, in Oran, his mother, Lucienne Mathieu-Saint-Laurent, glued his first sketches, his first words, and articles about his first successes in a notebook that she gave to him.

COUTURE

Album d'Yves-

CET ETUDIANT ORANAIS
REÇOIT (Aujourd'hui aux Ambassadeurs) LE 3e PRIX
AU « GONCOURT DU DESSIN DE MODE »

TOUT dernièrement a eu lieu à Paris l'attribution d'un nouveau prix que certains journaux n'ont pas hésité à appeler le « Goncourt du dessin de mode ».

C'est en effet au cours d'un déjeuner chez Maxim's, que les grands couturiers Christian Dior, Jacques Fath et Hubert de Givenchy, assistés de Jacqueline Delubac, du peintre Jean Oberlé et de M. Gruau ont décerné le prix du concours de dessin de mode, organisé par le secrétariat international de la laine. Ces diverses personnalités étaient entourées de plusieurs représentants de la presse et de l'élégance : Michel Brunhoff, directeur du journal « Vogue » ; Mmes Simone Baron, de « Elle », et de Souza, du « Figaro ».

Le concours était ouvert à tous ceux et celles qui, sans avoir d'attache avec la haute couture et la presse spécialisée, ont le sens de l'élégance et le goût du dessin. Il s'agissait de créer des modèles de manteau, tailleur et robe. Une seule condition était imposée : ces modèles devaient être conçus pour être réalisés en tissus de laine.

Les candidats furent nombreux et les organisateurs reçurent près de 9.000 dessins, qu'un pré-jury examina avec soin, ne retenant en dernier lieu qu'une quinzaine de modèles qui furent soumis au jury, dont nous avons indiqué ci-dessus la composition.

C'est ainsi qu'un jeune étudiant oranais, Yves Mathieu Saint-Laurent, âgé seulement de 17 ans, se vit attribuer le troisième prix, pour un modèle présenté dans la catégorie « Robes ».

Le jeune lauréat est un grand garçon, un peu timide, que son succès effrale plutôt qu'il ne le grise. Nous avons voulu connaître ses réactions et aussi ses projets d'avenir après ce premier succès, qui est en quelque sorte une consécration officielle de son talent.

Yves Mathieu Saint-Laurent

Depuis son jeune âge, Yves Mathieu Saint-Laurent s'intéresse au dessin. Il a déjà exécuté maints dessins, portraits, esquisses qui révèlent un goût sûr et exquis. A l'âge de 12 ans, il illustrait des romans célèbres et dans le domaine de la mode a créé plus d'un millier de modèles.

— Comment Yves Mathieu Saint-Laurent, avez-vous eu l'idée de participer à ce concours ?

— En en lisant l'annonce dans l'hebdomadaire « Paris-Match ». J'ai dessiné plusieurs modèles pour chacune des catégories indiquées. Le règlement prévoyait l'exécution du dessin en noir et blanc, d'un format de 30 centimètres sur 20. En outre, il fallait joindre un échantillon du tissu, en laine naturellement, prévu pour la confection. J'ai ainsi envoyé sans grande conviction mes travaux au jury, et je suis aussi surpris qu'heureux du résultat.

— Les dessins que vous avez déjà exécutés, autres que les croquis de mode, sont-ils inspirés de modèles ?

— Jusqu'à présent, je me suis laissé guider par mon imagination, quel que soit le genre de dessin.

— Quels sont vos projets d'avenir ? Je pense que ce succès aura quelque influence sur ceux-ci ?

— J'ai toujours eu l'intention de faire de la décoration et plus particulièrement de peindre des décors de théâtre. J'espère pouvoir suivre mes études à Paris afin de me perfectionner et de débuter au plus tôt dans cette voie.

Pour notre part, nous ne doutons pas que le jeune lauréat réussisse dans la carrière qu'il a choisie, et tous nos vœux l'accompagneront lorsqu'il partira, à Paris, à la conquête de la gloire, qui a d'ailleurs déjà commencé à lui sourire.

Aujourd'hui, 20 décembre, Yves Mathieu Saint-Laurent doit recevoir son prix, au cours d'une réception organisée aux Ambassadeurs.

Novembre 1953.

Robe de cocktail
à drapé asymétrique
Boutonnie de Jais

Beret de velours
rubis noué de
tulle gris perle

Ce dessin vaut à M.
Yves Mathieu Saint Laurent
le 1er prix (500.000 frs)
de la catégorie "robe"

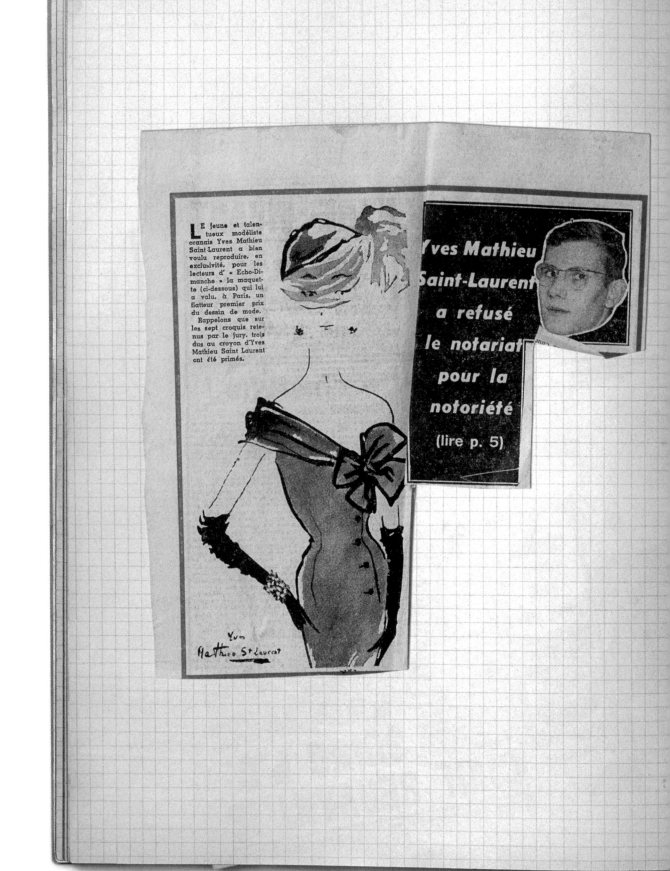

LE jeune et talentueux modéliste oranais Yves Mathieu Saint-Laurent a bien voulu reproduire, en exclusivité, pour les lecteurs d' « Echo-Dimanche » la maquette (ci-dessous) qui lui a valu, à Paris, un flatteur premier prix du dessin de mode.

Rappelons que sur les sept croquis retenus par le jury, trois dus au crayon d'Yves Mathieu Saint Laurent ont été primés.

Yves Mathieu Saint-Laurent a refusé le notariat pour la notoriété

(lire p. 5)

PARCE QU'IL NE VOULAIT PAS ÊTRE NOTAIRE

L'Oranais Y. Mathieu SAINT-LAURENT sera (peut-être) un grand couturier

ORAN est à l'honneur en la personne d'Yves Saint-Laurent qui vient de remporter à l'unanimité le premier prix du Concours organisé, à Paris par le Secrétariat de la Laine, concours destiné, rappelons-le à récompenser le meilleur dessin de mode exécuté par un amateur.

Yves Saint-Laurent n'est pas un inconnu pour nos lecteurs. L'an dernier, il remportait déjà le troisième prix de ce concours que l'on qualifie, injustement, de « Goncourt de la Mode » puisque tous les envois sont strictement anonymes.

Cette année, son talent s'impose avec autorité. Dans chaque catégorie — robes, tailleurs, manteaux — trois prix furent décernés or il s'est trouvé que sur les sept croquis « robes » soumis en dernier ressort au jury, trois d'entre eux étaient l'œuvre d'Yves Saint-Laurent. Deux furent primés à l'unanimité... C'est un beau résultat.

Nous sommes allés interviewer le jeune lauréat. Il a dix-huit ans, un physique d'étudiant de Sciences Pô — sérieux et réservé et des idées révolutionnaires en matière de mode.

— « L'élégance dit-il, c'est une robe trop éblouissante pour oser la porter deux fois. J'aime l'excentrique, le drôle, l'inattendu.

— Les couturiers que j'admire : Balenciaga et Hubert de Givenchy. C'est d'ailleurs ce dernier

qui va exécuter ma robe, je suis comblé !

— Etiez-vous donc sûr de gagner ?

— Non, sans doute, mettons que j'avais un pressentiment »

Venu à Paris au mois d'octobre Yves Saint-Laurent, parrainé depuis le concours de l'an dernier par Michel De Brunhoff Directeur de « Vogue », suit actuellement des cours de coupe à la Chambre Syndicale de la couture. Il préfère créer qu'exécuter. Dans un an il aura terminé.

— Que comptez-vous faire ensuite ?...

— Mon rêve serait d'être modéliste dans une grande maison de Couture... Oh, créer des robes gaies, vivantes sur lesquelles on se retourne, imaginer des accessoires audacieux, de ces bijoux « couture » qui sont tellement plus spirituels que les vrais...

— La mode mise à part, quelle autre carrière vous tenterait ?

— Le théâtre qui en est un peu le prolongement : dessiner des décors, des costumes de scène... être sans cesse en contact avec ce public qui encense ou qui condamne.

— Comment votre famille a-t-elle accueilli votre succès ?

— Mon père qui appartient à une vieille famille de notaires oranais, ne croyait guère au début à ma « vocation ». Aujourd'hui il se résigne et accepte que je sois « l'artiste de la famille »

Un sourire éclaire son visage sérieux. Un sourire qu'aucun photographe n'a pu saisir car Yves Saint-Laurent s'il aime les robes audacieuses, les couleurs bruyantes et les chapeaux extravagants est un garçon timide que rien n'effraie comme la publicité que lui vaut son jeune et incontestable talent.

Janie SAMET

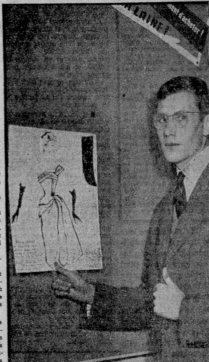

Le jeune lauréat Yves SAINT LAURENT tient ici le croquis qui lui a valu le troisième prix catégorie robe : robe de cocktail en algouleine noir dont le drapé est fixé à la taille par un clip de s...

...t l'oreille...

MOMENT CRUCIAL

Le jury du concours de dessins de mode organisé par le Secrétariat International de la Laine, est en train de délibérer. On reconnaît de gauche à droite : M. Simoni, qui représente la maison Jacques Fath, bavardant avec notre collaboratrice Françoise Brénon, Hubert de Givenchy qui exécutera la robe primée, M. Weber, directeur du Secrétariat International de la Laine, Pierre Balmain et M. Lesur. Au premier rang, Jacqueline Delubac examine un croquis.

Voici les croquis primés fixés sur un écran

DAMES

2ème concours de dessins de mode du secrétariat international de la laine

C'est M. Bernard Lafay, président du Conseil municipal de Paris, qui a remis le montant de leurs récompenses aux lauréats du concours de dessins de mode organisé pour la deuxième année consécutive, par le Secrétariat international de la Laine. La réunion s'est déroulée dans une salle des Champs-Elysées et la grande presse, la radio, le cinéma, la télévision y assistaient. En même temps qu'elle apportait la notoriété à des talents, la veille encore inconnus, elle a illustré, une fois de plus cette vérité incontestée que Paris est la capitale de l'élégance féminine.

Un titre que lui conserve l'inspiration, sans cesse renouvelée, de ses jeunes artistes, de ses grands couturiers — et aussi de ces autres créateurs que, dans sa brillante improvisation M. Bernard Lafay a appelé ses « marchands ». En l'espèce, c'étaient les lainiers, ceux qui fournissent à la Haute Couture la matière première dans laquelle ses idées revêtent leur forme sensible. En rendant hommage aux « marchands » de Paris, le Président du Conseil rappela que, par ses fonctions, il est aujourd'hui le successeur de leurs prévôts et que nombre de ces prévôts, parmi lesquels Etienne Marcel, ont appartenu à la puissante et importante corporation de la Laine.

Odette Joyeux avait écrit l'a-propos qui anima la manifestation. Elle s'y était réservée le rôle de Pénélope et Jacques Charon, de la Comédie Française lui donnait la réplique, avec deux élèves du Conservatoire. La fin du sketch amena le public à acclamer les noms de Pierre Balmain, de Jacques Fath et d'Hubert de Givenchy Il ne resta plus qu'à faire venir sur le podium les mannequins qui présentaient les modèles réalisés par ces grands couturiers d'après les dessins récompensés par les trois « premier prix » du concours — ces dessins ayant été choisis parmi quelques six mille envois.

C'était Pierre Balmain qui avait exécuté, dans un tissu de laine jaune poussin (de chez Gérondeau), le manteau de cocktail conçu par M. Karl O. Lagerfeld, premier prix de la catégorie « manteau ». Le modèle qui avait valu à Mlle Colette Bracchi le premier prix de la catégorie « tailleur », avait été exécuté par les ateliers de Jacques Fath en tissu de laine noir (de chez Pétillault) pour la jupe et en gros tissu de laine blanc (de chez Lesur) pour la veste. Enfin, la robe de cocktail de M. Yves Mathieu Saint Laurent, premier prix de la catégorie « robe » avait été exécutée par Hubert de Givenchy dans un tissu de laine noir (de chez Rodier).

Robe de cocktail à drapé asymétrique, boutonnée de jais.
Béret de velours rubis noué de tulle gris perle.
Ce dessin vaut à M. Yves Mathieu Saint-Laurent (d'Oran) le 1er prix (300.000 fr.) de la catégorie «robe»

Le concours, on le sait, avait pour objet de donner leur chance à de jeunes dessinateurs et dessinatrices encore inconnus et en même temps de démontrer une fois de plus que les tissus de laine répondent à toutes les exigences de la virtuosité et de la technique des grands couturiers. L'accueil que le public a fait aux modèles réalisés d'après les trois meilleurs dessins prouve que, sur ces deux points, il a rempli son office. En remettant à chacun des jeunes lauréats (le plus jeune a 18 ans, l'aînée, 22) un chèque de 300.000 francs, M. Bernard Lafay n'a pas jugé imprudent de leur dire qu'ils étaient « sur la route du succès ». Il ne se trompait pas puisque l'un d'entre eux, au moins, a déjà été pressenti pour collaborer avec le grand couturier qui a exécuté son modèle.

Dans chacune des catéories «manteau», «robe» et «tailleur», deux autres prix de 100.000 et de 50.000 francs, avaient également été décernés. C'est aussi M. Bernard Lafay qui les a remis à leurs bénéficiaires en leur souhaitant de faire encore mieux une autre année.

En quoi, s'ils y parviennent, ils ne feront que suivre l'exemple de M. Yves Mathieu Saint Laurent et de Mlle Colette Bracchi. Tous deux, en effet, avant de triompher dans le concours de 1954, avaient déjà tenté leur chance dans le concours de 1953, et s'y étaient respectivement classés en troisième et quatrième position dans la catégorie « robe ». Ce qui prouve que pour réussir, il faut d'abord, bien sûr, avoir des dons, mais aussi les cultiver.

M. Yves Mathieu Saint-Laurent, 1er prix catégorie "robe"

M. Yves Mathieu Saint-Laurent, lui, (premier prix de la catégorie "robe") appartient à une famille d'avocats bien connue à Oran. Il est maintenant âgé de 18 ans. Il avait pris part déjà l'année dernière au premier concours de dessins de Mode et son envoi lui avait valu un troisième prix dans la catégorie "robe". Il vivait alors chez ses parents à Oran et était venu à Paris pour y recevoir le montant de sa récompense qui lui avait été remis (déjà) aux Ambassadeurs, par Mme Jacqueline Delubac. Encouragé par ce premier succès, il s'était peu après fixé dans la capitale pour y travailler, lui aussi, le dessin à l'école de la Chambre Syndicale de la Haute Couture. La robe qu'il a conçue est une robe de cocktail. Elle a été exécutée en lainage noir (de chez Rodier) par Hubert de Givenchy. M. Saint-Laurent est le grand triomphateur du concours de cette année puisqu'un autre de ses envois lui vaut également le troisième prix de la catégorie "robe". (Il convient de souligner à ce propos que, si les chroniqueurs de Mode, l'année dernière, ont spontanément baptisé le concours "Goncourt de la Mode", le jury dudit concours, contrairement à celui du vrai Goncourt, classe les envois sans connaître leurs auteurs. Les dessins qui lui sont présentés ne portent qu'un numéro. Seul, l'huissier qui les a centralisés, est en mesure de retrouver les noms de leurs auteurs. Il ne les révèle aux jurés que lorsque leur choix est définitivement arrêté.)

Un modéliste oranais remporte le « Prix International de la Laine »

Journal d'Alger 11 décembre

LA COUTURE A AUSSI SON SAINT LAURENT

Le « Secrétariat international d... la Laine » a créé un concours annuel de figurines de mode, dont les prix viennent d'être attribués pour la seconde année. Il s'agit de proposer des modèles, exécutables en lainage, dans trois catégories de vêtements : manteaux, tailleurs et robes. Chaque catégorie étant dotée de trois prix, respectivement de 300.000, 100.000 et 50.000 francs, ce qui fait un total de 1 million 350.000 francs, il y a de quoi stimuler les concurrents. Ils étaient 6.000 cette année. Fait étonnant, un étudiant oranais qui l'an dernier, s'était classé troisième de la catégorie « robe », à 17 ans, vient de cumuler, cette fois-ci, le premier et le troisième prix du même groupe. Il s'était d'ailleurs fixé à Paris.

Trois jeunes gens, lauréats d'un concours de dessins de mode gagnent 300.000 fr.

Les trois lauréats d'un concours, qui avait pour objet de donner leurs chances à de jeunes dessinateurs de modes encore inconnus, ont reçu, hier soir, des mains de M. Bernard Lafay, président du Conseil municipal de Paris, le chèque de 300.000 francs qui récompensait le jeune talent.

Mlle Colette Bracchi, 22 ans, d'origine italienne ; M. Yves Mathieu Saint-Laurent, 18 ans, d'Oran, et M. Karl Lagerfeld, 21 ans, de Hambourg, ont prouvé une fois de plus, en gagnant respectivement les premiers prix des catégories : tailleur, robe, manteau, qu'une idée venant de Paris obtient toujours une audience internationale.

La remise des prix de ce concours, organisé pour la deuxième fois par le secrétariat international de la laine, se déroulait dans les salons d'un grand restaurant de l'avenue Gabriel. De nombreuses personnalités du monde de la mode ont acclamé longuement les créations de Hubert de Givenchy, de Pierre Balmain, du regretté Jacques Fath, réalisées d'après les dessins des jeunes lauréats qui peuvent, sans aucun doute, entrevoir, dès à présent, l'espoir d'une brillante carrière dans la haute couture.

Un jeune modéliste oranais, M. Yves Mathieu Saint-Laurent, vient d'être révélé au grand public et de connaître la consécration en remportant le « Prix International de la Laine », qui mettait aux prises une centaine de modélistes représentant vingt pays. Les modèles primés ont été exécutés dans les ateliers des grands couturiers parisiens. La catégorie « manteaux » a vu triompher un Allemand, M. Karl Lagerfeld, et la catégorie « tailleurs » une Italienne, Mlle Colette Bracchi. M. Mathieu Saint-Laurent, qui a permis à la France de remporter le grand prix de la catégorie « robes », n'a cela mérite d'être souligné — que 18 ans.

LES INDISCRÉTIO...

Chez Maxim's, hier, au cours d'un déjeuner, les lauréats du concours de croquis de mode (organisé par le Secrétariat international de la Laine) ont été désignés par un jury composé de M. Weber, Mme Switenburg, Jacqueline Delubac, Pierre Balmain, Hubert de Givenchy ; M. Simoni, représentant la maison Jacques Fath, et quelques journalistes.

M. Yves Saint-Laurent, dix-huit ans, obtint le premier prix « robe » avec un croquis qui sera réalisé par Givenchy. La maison Fath traduira le croquis de tailleur de Colette Bracchi, vingt et un ans, et Pierre Balmain interprétera le manteau de Carl Lagerfeld, Parisien de vingt-deux ans.

Le mois prochain, les créations primées seront présentées par des mannequins.

Sur notre document, on distingue (marqués d'une X et de gauche à droite) MM. Simoni et Givenchy, Mme Delubac et M. Balmain.

UTURS ESPOIRS
e la Haute-Couture

Deux jeunes gens et une jeune fille de 18 à
ans viennent de remporter plus d'un million
prix en faisant le concours de dessins de mode
anisé par le Secrétariat international de la laine.
Il s'agit de Mlle Colette Bracchi, qui remporte
premier prix dans la catégorie « Tailleur » ; de
Yves Mathieu Saint-Laurent, premier prix de
atégorie « Robe », et enfin, de M. Karl O. Lager-
, premier prix de la catégorie « Manteau ».

Ce concours, on le sait, avait pour but de donner
chance à de jeunes dessinateurs et dessinatrices
re inconnus et de démontrer que les tissus de
e répondent à toutes les exigences de la virtuosité
e la technique des grands couturiers.

Au cours d'une soirée très brillante, présentée
Jacques Charron, de la Comédie-Française, le
out Paris » de l'élégance applaudit les jeunes
urrents qui reçurent des mains de M. Bernard
y, président du Conseil municipal de Paris, les
ues venant récompenser leur talent.

Voici les lauréats avec la réalisation de leurs
ns : (de gauche à droite) MM. Karl, O. Lager-
(manteau), Yves Mathieu Saint-Laurent (robe)
Mlle Colette Bracchi (tailleur).

Le concours de dessins de mode

Un étudiant de 18 ans réalise une double performance

TROIS étudiants, dont l'aîné a vingt et un ans, et six jeunes femmes ou jeunes filles de vingt à trente-cinq ans (on trouvera plus loin leurs noms et leurs adresses) se partageront les 1.350.000 francs de prix du concours de dessins de mode organisé pour la deuxième année consécutive par le Secrétariat International de la Laine. L'épreuve, on le sait, a pour but de donner leur chance à de jeunes dessinateurs (ou dessinatrices) encore inconnus et en même temps de démontrer, une fois de plus, que les tissus de laine leur permet de satisfaire toutes les exigences de la virtuosité des grands couturiers.

Deux conditions étaient donc imposées aux concurrents : ils ne devaient pas être (ou avoir été) attachés à des journaux de mode ou à des maisons de couture, et ils ne devaient concevoir que des modèles destinés à être exécutés dans des tissus de laine. Trois « catégories » étaient prévues : robe, tailleur et manteau, le montant des récompenses étant, dans chacune de ces catégories, de 300.000 francs pour le lauréat classé premier, de 100.000 fr pour le second, et de 50.000 francs pour le troisième.

Le grand triomphateur du concours de cette année est un jeune étudiant de dix-huit ans, M. Yves-Mathieu Saint-Laurent qui, dans la catégorie robe, remporte deux prix, le premier et le troisième. Il convient de souligner à ce propos que, si les chroniqueurs de mode, l'année dernière, ont spontanément baptisé le concours « Goncourt de la Mode », le jury dudit concours, contrairement à celui du vrai Goncourt, classe les envois sans connaître leurs auteurs. Les dessins qui lui sont présentés ont été rassemblés par un huissier et ne portent qu'un numéro. C'est seulement après la proclamation des résultats que l'huissier — en l'occurrence Me Agnus — recherche, dans ses fiches, le nom des auteurs des dessins et les révèle aux jurés.

Le succès de M. Yves-Mathieu Saint-Laurent est à la fois logique et remarquable. Remarquable parce que M. Saint-Laurent n'a que dix-huit ans et que le fait que ses envois ont retenu deux fois l'attention du jury prouve que leur qualité n'est pas seulement due à un caprice de son inspiration. Et logique parce qu'il constitue aussi une confirmation. On n'a peut-être pas oublié, en effet, qu'en 1953 déjà, M. Yves-Mathieu Saint-Laurent avait pris part au premier concours de dessins de mode du Secrétariat International de la Laine et que, déjà, il avait obtenu un prix plus modeste — le troisième — dans la catégorie robe. Il habitait alors chez ses parents, à Oran, et il était venu à Paris pour recevoir timidement, aux Ambassadeurs, des mains de Mme Jacqueline Delubac, le montant de sa récompense. Ce premier succès l'a encouragé à se fixer à Paris pour y continuer ses études de dessin. S'il doutait de lui, la distinction dont il vient d'être l'objet lui prouverait qu'en un an il a fait des progrès. Il a réalisé aussi, soit dit en passant, une bonne opération en ne remportant pas un premier prix dès l'année dernière car, s'il l'avait fait, il se serait interdit — le règlement le stipulait — de prendre part à l'épreuve de cette année et d'y réussir une double performance.

LES LAUREATS

CATEGORIE ROBE :

1er et 3e prix : M. Yves-Mathieu Saint-Laurent, étudiant, dix-huit ans, chez Mme Buisson, 209, bd Péreire, Paris (XVIIe).

2e prix : Mlle Godet, vingt-deux ans, étudiante, 27, rue de la Py, Paris (XXe).

CATEGORIE MANTEAU :

1er prix : M. Karl O. Lagerfeld, vingt et un ans, étudiant, 14, rue de la Sorbonne, Paris (Ve).

2e prix : M. Hervé Dubly, dix-neuf ans, étudiant, 4, rue de Musset, Paris (XVIe).

3e prix : Mlle Geneviève Talmon, 27 ans, sans profession, chez la comtesse Rubini, 18, r. Montalivet Paris-VIIIe.

CATEGORIE TAILLEUR :

1er prix : Mlle Colette Bracchi, vingt-deux-ans, 18, boulevard Montmartre, Paris (IXe).

2e Prix : Mme P. Brumpt, sans profession, 51, av. de la Motte-Piquet, Paris (XVe).

3e prix : Mlle Jane Cobessi, vingt et un ans, étudiante, 54, avenue de Paris Villejuif (Seine).

TROIS ESPOIRS

LES trois lauréats du concours de dessins de mode organisé par le Secrétariat International de la Laine, à Paris. Ce concours avait pour but de donner leur chance à de jeunes artistes inconnus qui devaient démontrer que les tissus de laine répondent à toutes les exigences de l'élégance. Sur notre document, de gauche à droite : M. Karl Lagerfeld et son manteau exécuté dans les ateliers de Pierre Balmain ; M. Yves-Mathieu Saint-Laurent et sa robe exécutée par les soins d'Hubert de Givenchy et Mlle Colette Bracchi ajustant son tailleur sur un mannequin de la maison Jacques Fath qui réalisa son œuvre.

HACE veinte años, jóvenes modelistas desconocidos se incorporaban a las casas que un día llevarían su nombre. Se llamaban Pierre Balmain, Balenciaga, Christian Dior, Jacques Fath... Hoy, otros "jóvenes turcos" perpetúan la tradición de talento e inquietud de la Alta Costura francesa. Algunos de entre ellos han alcanzado ya su éxito; los modelos que ellos crearon llevan su firma. Otros animan anónimamente casas que no son las suyas. Y todavía otros, encerrados en pequeños apartamentos, logran hallazgos maravillosos, y esperan al más importante de los clientes, la oportunidad.

Este reportaje está consagrado a estos "benjamines". Presentamos aquí a los que han logrado plenamente su éxito, a los que están al borde de conseguirlo, a los que han optado trabajar para los demás, y a los que en un estudio de un último piso preparan los "fuegos artificiales" que quizá les hagan célebres mañana.

Paul Poiret terminó en la miseria. Las jóvenes de 1957 recuerdan apenas los nombres gloriosos de Worth y de Paquin. Pero la aureola de gloria de un Fath o de un Dior es lo bastante fabulosa como para que un numeroso grupo de jóvenes se sienta violentamente atraído por uno de los oficios más difíciles del mundo. La elección por el equipo "Cristian Dior", de Yves Mathieu Saint-Laurent, como modelista número uno de la gran casa de la avenida Montaigne, constituye una de las más grandes oportunidades ofrecidas a los jóvenes impacientes de Alta Costura.

¡El rey ha muerto, vivan los delfines!

Yves Saint-Laurent ha resultado el "heredero" de Christian Dior. Pero al lado del "delfín" figura también M... Raymond, que ha trabajado a su lado en los talleres de la avenue Montaigne.

LOS «BENJA...

llevada como hasta ahora; la responsabilidad, compartida por todos los que rodearon a Dior a lo largo de casi toda su carrera. Pero por encima de esto destaca la aparición de este nuevo astro de la Alta Costura.

Como él se encuentran varios otros que no han tenido tan fabulosa oportunidad. Ganan entre 150 y 200.000 francos por mes, contando con una pequeñísima participación en los be-

hubiera recaído una corona demasiado pesada. Yves Saint-Laurent ha nacido en el año 1936, en Orán, y conoció a Dior en el año 1953, con ocasión de un concurso de dibujo, al que asistía como jurado, y del que se llevó a este muchacho que hoy

● Jules François Crahay tien... la edad que Dior tenía cuan... abandonó a Lelong para fun... propia casa. A los cuarenta... Crahay es el único modelista... na Ricci. Madame Nina Ricc... para una cuarta parte de la co... y él lo restante; tiene muchas... que no puede poner en práctica... cuadro un poco 1900 de esta cas... "rue de Capucines". Era belga y... patria empezó en la profesión, pe... firió pasar la frontera y ahora... dido su naturalización.

TRES TRIUNFADORES: GIVE...
LAROCHE Y CARDIN

TRES que han triunfado: Gi... Laroche y Cardin. Los tres... un gran talento, ideas jóvenes... vas. Los tres han tenido tamb... oportunidad. Givenchy, la de ser... do por Balenciaga; Cardin, la de... der su oficio en la casa Dior; L... el temerario, la de haber osado in... se sin capital.

Hubert de Givenchy, el más... ideas, es también el más joven (... años) y el más "grande" (dos... cuatro centímetros). Cuando se l... la aventura, el 3 de febrero de 19... era más que un joven y turbulen... delista de Schiaparelli. En su ho... parque Monceau, bajo los "plafon... pertenecieron a una chocolatería... talado estrechamente, desde las... gas al granero, a sus ciento se... cinco obreros, sus diez vendedoras... co maniquíes. Estas cifras son... tas cuando se las compara con... nombre. Hubert de Givenchy adm... un discípulo de Balenciaga y se... que ambos se reúnen para discuti... parar las próximas colecciones.

Como Balenciaga, Givenchy ti... clientes a las mujeres más "sno... mundo; es el maestro del negro y... vestidos extraordinariamente co... dos en su aparente simplicidad. S... ha dicho que Audrey Hepburn es... jer que prefiere vestir. También... Balenciaga, ha escogido la publi... misterio y se ha rodeado de un s... te muy "gran siglo": Bach,... Luis XVI... El no será jamás e... de un imperio, como lo era Dior... de decidir la largura de los ves... difundirla e imponerla por los ci... tinentes.

● Guy Laroche ha triunfado... tuvo el valor de llamar casa... das a un pasillo. En un piso inst...

LOS SUCESORES DE LOS "GRANDES" DE LA ALTA COSTURA HAN CONSEGUIDO SU MEJOR VICTORIA
YVES SAINT-LAURENT, HEREDERO DE DIOR

EN UNA CASA QUE NO LLEVA SU NOMBRE

JORNADA histórica en la casa Dior. El testamento del creador del "new-look" ha sido hecho público: la colección Dior 1958 será firmada por Yves Saint-Laurent. La dirección de la casa será

le ha sucedido. Ahora espera al mes de febrero con confianza e impaciencia. Esta maravillosa máquina Dior, que funciona desde hace diez años, siendo a la vez laboratorio, estudio y teatro, está ahora en las manos de un muchacho, que ya tiene de común con su padrino llevar uno de los más conocidos nombres de Francia. Tiene el trono de oro de los reyes, va a sentarse en él con cierto miedo.

neficios cuantiosos que dejan las colecciones. Esto no es ni la gloria ni la fortuna, pero es la seguridad, y puede ser la esperada oportunidad.

Esta le ha llegado en la casa Dior al "discípulo preferido", el cual el día de su designación tenía el aire de un joven príncipe sobre el que

● Es porque perdió, a los ocho años, un brazo, por lo que se ha convertido en modista Jean Pomarède. No podía seguir siendo el jefe de banda de muchachos del pequeño pueblecito vasco en el que había nacido, y se convirtió en el acompañante fiel y triste de dos ancianas señoras. Las guardaba las ropas, revolvía entre sus vestidos, jugaba con sus paraguas.

Esto, quizá, es lo que le hizo dedicarse a este trabajo. Entró en la casa Lelong —donde trabajó con Christian Dior— y después, desde hace ocho años, en el negocio de Jacques Heim, donde se convirtió rápidamente en el animador de la casa. Jean Pomarède apenas dibuja, y, según él, lo hace "bastante mal", prefiriendo trabajar sobre un maniquí vivo que sobre las cuartillas.

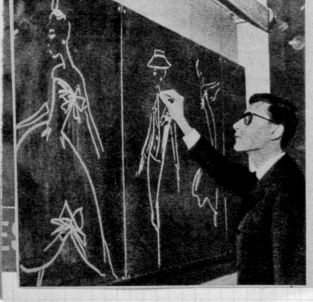

◄ Yves Saint-Laurent muestra gráficamente, y en una pizarra, su estilo de diseñador.

necesario para lanzarse a la gran ...tura. En la cocina situó "sus talle- ...La entrada, que tiene un largo pa- ...como tantas casas particulares, la ...onvertido en salón de exhibiciones. ...operarios no los contrata, los al- ...; él adorna sus muros, instala la ...ricidad y compra tela de colchón ...hacer las cortinas. Tampoco puede ...atar maniquíes, sino que lleva un ...de horas al día a algunas de las ...bellas muchachas de París. Ellas ...n confianza en él y algunas se han ...después, como Marie Helene Ar- ...y Ghiseline Arsac, sobre las cu- ...as de "Life". En dos horas de des- ...nada más inaugurar su casa, se ...erte en la mascota de París. Su

solución más fácil: la confección, me- nos exigente y más generosa.

● Marc Bohan ha tenido su casa. Después estuvo cuatro años en Patóu, únicamente como creador. Desde hace dos meses diseña para un confeccionador suizo. Tiene los ojos un poco tristes, del muchacho a quien se le ha privado de su sueño. Marc Bohan está muy brillante- mente dotado. Su antepenúltima co- lección de alta costura, presentada en el mes de febrero último, fué qui- zá la más bella de París. En 1953 se había instalado en la avenida Geor- ge V, con dos talleres, cuatro vende- doras y poco dinero. Pero no tuvo la fuerza financiera necesaria para pasar el invierno.

ES» DE LA MODA

...ra colección —sesenta modelos— fué ...iunfo. Desde entonces la empera- ...oraya, Michèle Morgan, Bobo Roc- ...er, la mujer de Onassis, Lily Pons ...chas otras han subido esa escale- ...la que ningún portero galoneado ...la puerta. ...ra ellas, como para todas sus clien- ...as vendedoras han instalado en el ...o-salón de exhibición unas cortinas ...a de colchón. Así ha nacido una ...de pruebas. ...América, Guy Laroche es ahora ...célebre. Ha pagado sus deudas e ...stalado dos apartamentos nuevos, ...s que trabajan sus cuatro talleres. ...emplazado su Simca por un Thun- ...d. Lanzará, para Navidad, su pri- ...erfume. Pero no abrirá tienda el ...; se considera un superartesano.

OS QUE HAN ESCOGIDO LA CONFECCION

Y quienes han tentado su opor- ...nidad y la han encontrado. Pero ...ién hay quienes han retrocedido ...las enormes dificultades que re- ...ar. Han escogido, en definitiva, la

● Alwyn fué un relámpago ful- gurante en el cielo de la alta costura hace siete años. A su pri- mera colección este muchacho de veinticuatro años sorprendió a to- dos los compradores norteameri- canos, pero no supo mantenerse, y la segunda no fué el estallido que había sido la primera. Abandonó la costura de la misma manera que la había abordado. Hace ahora deco- rados y trajes para el cine, el teatro y los cabarets.

● Después de la muerte de Fath, de quien era uno de los mode- listas preferidos, Max Sarian ha en- trado en unos grandes almacenes. Hace ahora vestidos simples y elegan- tes, de los que algunos parecen sa- lidos de la tienda de algún modista. Dior, que le apreciaba mucho, le ofre- ció trabajar para su firma, pero las condiciones que le proponía no re- presentaban más que la mitad de lo que conseguía como primer modelis- ta de una gran casa de confección; después de haber dudado mucho, re- husó la proposición de Dior. Le habrá pesado, a bien seguro; pero en su terreno él ha triunfado. Aporta verdadera elegancia a muje-

res que no han cruzado jamás la puerta de una casa de modas.

LOS QUE ESPERAN LA OPOR- TUNIDAD

JACQUES Heduy, como Christian Dior, ha estudiado ciencias polí- ticas. Como él, también no tenía nin-

gún interés por la inspección o las embajadas. Ha comenzado en un pe- queño local de dos habitaciones cer- ca del parque Monceau; pero los clientes han ido llegando y hoy se ha instalado en un gran apartamento del "faubourg" Saint-Honoré. A los treinta y cinco años está lleno de op-

El boceto creado por Yves Saint-Laurent tuvo largo esa expresión real, ex- hibida por una modelo de Christian Dior.

timismo, vende sus modelos entre treinta y cinco mil y ochenta mil francos. Su situación no es florecien- te, pero espera ascender de año en año hasta llegar a ser un día uno de los "grandes".

● Como él, Jacques Fougeirol, de veintiocho años, que ha llegado a la moda por las artes decorativas. Muy personal, asegura que "lo que hacen los otros le deja indiferente". Todos esperan ser un día de los grandes; algunos lo conseguirán, otros, desanimados, renunciarán. Son muchas decenas en París, unos apren- diendo todavía su oficio con un mo- disto, otros ya lanzados; han abier- to, quizá, una casa que puede con- sistir en dos habitaciones de un apartamento con fachada al Fau- bourg Saint-Honoré. Todos esperan su oportunidad.

Luis de ANJOU

‹ Hubert de Givenchy, desde su imponente altu- ra, anuncia su dominio sobre el futuro de la moda.

Les collaborateurs les plus proches de CHRISTIAN DIOR lui succéderont

La direction artistique est confiée au jeune dessinateur Yves-Mathieu SAINT-LAURENT

DEVANT toutes les journalistes de mode qu'il avait réunies hier, le directeur commercial de la maison Dior, M. Jacques Rouet, a confirmé la décision concernant la succession du grand couturier. Cette décision, nous l'avions déjà annoncée, il y a plusieurs jours : aucun étranger ne viendra prendre la tête de la maison de couture, dont la direction sera désormais assurée par ceux qui furent les plus proches collaborateurs de Christian Dior.

Mme Raymonde ZEHNACKER et M. Yves-Mathieu SAINT-LAURENT pendant la conférence de presse

C'était le désir du disparu que la maison Dior, cette extraordinaire réussite ne dépende pas de sa seule présence. Christian Dior avait créé une mode mais aussi une technique. Cette technique M. Yves-Mathieu Saint-Laurent, un tout jeune homme de vingt et un ans, l'a étudiée aux côtés du maître depuis quatre ans. A la suite d'un concours, en 1953, auquel il avait obtenu le premier prix, il était entré comme dessinateur chez Christian Dior dont il était le disciple préféré. C'est à lui qu'incombera désormais la direction artistique de la maison.

La direction de la création sera assurée par Mme Raymonde Zehnacker qui a collaboré avec le grand couturier depuis 1946, année de sa première collection. Elle sera secondée dans cette tâche par Mme Marguerite Carré, aussi ancienne qu'elle dans la maison. Enfin Mme Bricart continuera à diriger le rayon de chapeaux et d'accessoires.

Ainsi par l'intermédiaire de ces quatre personnes — Mme Raymonde, Mme Carré, Mme Bricart, M. Saint-Laurent — la maison Christian Dior poursuivra l'œuvre édifiée avec M. Marcel Boussac et continuera à imposer au monde son goût et son génie.

Yves-Mathieu SAINT-LAURENT succède à 21 ans, à Christian DIOR. Il se signala à l'attention en 1954, en remportant le premier prix d'un concours international de dessin. Peu après, il entrait chez DIOR en qualité de modéliste et devenait bientôt le plus proche collaborateur du grand couturier. Le voici, en 1954, présentant au cours d'une soirée aux Ambassadeurs, la robe réalisée d'après son dessin primé. (A.D.P.)

YVES-MATHIEU SAINT-LAURENT préparera la prochaine collection Dior

LE directeur de la Société Christian Dior, M. Rouet, a donné une conférence de presse hier soir. C'est bien — comme cela se chuchotait depuis quelques jours dans les milieux parisiens bien informés — M. Yves-Mathieu Saint-Laurent qui reprend la succession artistique de Christian Dior. Ce dernier, qui pensait être obligé de se retirer, avait commencé à former ce jeune modéliste. Il sera entouré de l'ancien état-major de Dior : Mmes Raymonde Zenacker, Marguerite Carré et Bricard.

CI-CONTRE : Yves-Mathieu Saint-Laurent et Mme Raymonde Zenacker.

Yves Mathieu-Saint-Laurent a reçu la consécration de Paris

Nous avons publié, dans notre numéro d'hier, un résumé de la conférence de presse donnée vendredi chez Christian Dior, et au cours de laquelle M. Jacques Rouet, directeur administratif et commercial, confirma que la direction artistique et technique de Christian Dior serait assurée par les plus fidèles collaborateurs du célèbre couturier. Il affirma, notamment, qu'Yves Mathieu-Saint-Laurent jouerait un rôle important dans le nouveau fonctionnement de la maison, puisqu'il est nommé adjoint à Mme Raymonde Zehnacker qui assurera la direction et la création.

Yves Mathieu-Saint-Laurent assumera, en effet, la responsabilité de créer la future collection.

Voici Yves Mathieu-Saint-Laurent et Mme Zehnacker pendant la conférence de presse où le jeune Oranais, mitraillé par les flashes, reçoit la consécration de la célébrité
(Interpress)

s collaborateurs directs de Christian Dior poursuivent son œuvre

Jacques Rouet, directeur ministratif et commercial de la on Christian Dior, a confirmé, après-midi, au cours d'une rence de presse, que la direction artistique et technique de la on Christian Dior serait assu- par les collaborateurs les plus es du célèbre couturier.

me Raymonde Zehnacker assu- la direction et la création, Mme Marguerite Carré.

Mme Raymonde » sera égale- secondée par Mme Bricard, particulier dans le domaine des eaux, et par Yves Mathieu- -Laurent, qui était devenu le borateur permanent de Chris- Dior pour la création et la aration de toutes les collec-.

direction administrative et nerciale continuera à être ée par M. Jacques Rouet.

Pluies diluviennes et orages sur la Tunisie

UX DIRECTRICES ccéder à Christian Dior

salons surchauf- Christian Dior et presse parisienne oquée au grand ues Rouet, gé- Christian Dior, é de presse (qui temps à New dans toutes les d'après lequel ale de Christian elon le vœu de ue sa carrière. la direction ar- tue de la célè- rée par « l'éco- participation de nacker qui, col- proche et la ristian Dior, est rice de la créa- rguerite Carré, n Dior dès la aison pour as- Dior. Elles Mme Bricard, é joué par elle

Tout le personnel de la maison, qui a conscience de constituer son école, espère donc se montrer digne de poursuivre l'œuvre de Christian Dior, qui avait porté le renom de la couture française dans le monde entier.

depuis le début de la maison, en particulier dans le domaine des chapeaux et des bijoux, et enfin par Yves Mathieu Saint-Laurent, disciple préféré de Christian Dior qui était devenu son collaborateur permanent pour la création et la préparation de toutes les collec- tions.

Yves Mathieu Saint Laurent
HAUTE COUTURE
PLACE-VENDÔME.

1ère Note des commandes de
MADAME de HENLé
:

1 ensemble Boutique jupe PULL } 30.000
MATIN. sac

1 Modèle grde collection. 70.000
" STANISLAS "

1 Modèle grde collection 60.000
" SHOGOUN " "chapeau 10.000

1 Modèle grde collection 80.000
" YOLANDA "

1 Modèle grde collection 150.000
" MATA HARI "

TOTAL   400.000 frs.

POUR PREPARER LA NOUVELLE COLLECTION DE DIOR

Yves Mathieu Saint-Laurent
Antée de la couture
est venu chercher l'inspiration
sur sa terre natale

Yves Mathieu Saint-Laurent accueilli par sa mère à l'aérodrome de La Sénia.

Tel Antée, Yves Mathieu Saint-Laurent a besoin de toucher la terre (natale) pour y puiser l'inspiration.

Ce n'est pas la première fois, depuis le début de sa jeune carrière qu'il revient passer quelque temps dans sa famille pour préparer, loin du bruit et de l'effervescence de Paris, la nouvelle collection. Mais depuis que sur ses épaules pèsent toutes les responsabilités de ce qui fut sous la direction de Christian Dior la première maison de couture de Paris, l'enjeu a pris une importance capitale.

La mode, c'est-à-dire l'allure, la couleur, la forme, des robes que porteront cet été les femmes les plus élégantes du monde entier, dépend un peu — et peut-être beaucoup — de ce qui germera dans l'esprit de ce grand garçon timide arrivé hier à La Sénia par l'avion d'Air France.

— Je n'ai rien à dire, a déclaré du bout des lèvres Yves Saint-Laurent comme une grande vedette qu'il est d'ailleurs devenu sans trop s'en rendre compte.

— Mais vous vous devez de dire quelque chose aux Oranais qui s'intéressent à vous », lui dis-je. J'ai bien senti que cette question comme les autres que j'ai posées ensuite pour meubler les blancs des réponses qui ne venaient pas, embarrassaient fort mon interlocuteur malgré lui.

Je sais que les tabous de la haute-couture comptent parmi les plus impératifs et je n'escomptais pas en vérité d'indiscrétion sur la ligne été 58. Mais peut-être aurions-nous pu avoir quelques confidences qui n'eussent pas enfreint le secret professionnel.

— Ce que je peux vous dire, confessa M. Saint-Laurent, c'est que je viens ici pour huit jours seulement dans le but de préparer ma collection. Voilà. »

Comme les grands réalisateurs, M. Saint-Laurent n'est pas bavard. Ce fut son mot de la fin.

Quelques instants après il retrouvait ses parents qui attendaient d'embrasser le jeune nouveau dieu de la couture.

J.-D. R.

Dans les salons de Dior où la ligne
« liane, longue et souple » a triomphé

La première à féliciter
Yves Saint-Laurent : sa mère

Mme Saint-Laurent, la mère du jeune couturier qui succède à Christian Dior, assistait, très émue et légèrement inquiète, à la présentation de la collection de printemps de son fils. Les chaleureux applaudissements qui saluaient l'apparition de chacun des tailleurs — véritables clous de la collection — amenaient petit à petit sur le visage de Mme Saint-Laurent une expression de joie et de confiance. Svelte et élégante dans un ensemble de lainage bleu vif, Mme Saint-Laurent a partagé avec son fils, à la fin du défilé, l'enthousiasme général.

A Paris, dans les salons de l'avenue Montaigne

TOUT PARIS
a salué
le talent
du jeune
YVES St-LAURENT
successeur
de Christian DIOR

EN PAGE 4 :
Le compte rendu
de notre envoyée spéciale
YRENE JAN

Dans les célèbres salons de l'avenue Montaigne, c'est un tout jeune modéliste au grand talent, Yves Mathieu Saint-Laurent qui succède, comme créateur, à Christian Dior (Actualités-Mondial-Photo)

LE SACRE DU
PRINTEMPS

Le rideau est levé sur la mode de printemps. Paris a perdu Christian Dior, Paris a consacré son successeur : Yves Saint-Laurent (ci-dessus) traçant la ligne « trapèze ». Lire p. 11 la présentation des collections nouvelles.

Yves SAINT-LAURENT triomphe chez DIOR avec ses marinières et ses vareuses de matelot

YVES SAINT-LAURENT vient de se tailler un succès sans précédent, sauf ceux de Christian Dior lui-même, en montrant une collection d'avant-garde où dominent la simplicité et la jeunesse, c'est-à-dire le style que toutes les femmes adorent.

Le « boom » a été sur les marinières marine, vraies vareuses de matelots, en lainage, ouvertes sur des plastrons blancs, pour les petits tailleurs, marine aussi, très souples, à peine blousants, à ceinture, et pour le brin de romantisme qui fleurit la mode : berthes plates ou plissées encadrant les épaules, robes de shantung ou de mousseline entièrement plissées, robes d'organdi. Bref, tout ce qui est jeune, simple et charmant.

LA MODE DE PRINTEMPS

CONSACRE UN NOUVEAU "NEW LOOK" :

Triomphe du "naturel"

Chez Christian DIOR

- Vestons
- Tricots de marin
- Plissés et blouses

JAMAIS deux sans trois »... Le troisième succès consécutif d'Yves Saint-Laurent « impose définitivement son talent de grand couturier. Décidant cette saison que la *ligne* céderait le pas au *style* et que ce style serait « naturel », c'est-à-dire souple, facile et jeune à l'extrême, il montre une silhouette à buste sinueux, taille à sa place, hanches effacées et dont le mot d'ordre est l'aisance.

Fait très important : le tailleur revient au classicisme... Coupé comme un veston d'homme mais plus court que celui-ci, il fleurit sa boutonnière d'un œillet ou d'un brin de muguet, et écarte délibérément du cou son col et ses revers dans un effet de « modestie » qui laisse largement apparaître le haut de la blouse ou de la robe. Plus courtes encore sont les vestes ceinturées de cuir, à jupes un peu évasées — un peu allongées aussi (40 cm. de terre). Troisième type de tailleur : celui dont la veste paraît coupée trop étroite et qui se porte ouverte, les devants n'arrivant pas à croiser. Intermédiaires entre le tailleur et la robe : les *deux-pièces vareuses* largement échancrées, comme celle du marin, sur la modestie ou sur un tricot à côtes blanc ; elles sont presque toujours en lainage marine.

Le nouveau manteau est un pardessus inédit : le *raspet*, qui est étroit, très « près du corps », boutonné haut, à col tailleur et manches montées. Galamment, il s'écourte toujours un peu pour permettre à la robe qu'il accompagne de se montrer.

Les robes du matin ont toutes des ceintures, mais — étourderie bien féminine — au moment où elles retrouvent leur taille, elles ont perdu leurs manches... Les bustes sont moulés et les jupes, même en gros lainage, souvent plissées. Elles annoncent déjà le triomphe du plissé dans les robes d'après-midi. Délaissant les jupons, celles-ci se plissent de l'épaule et tombent droites, resserrées souplement à la taille ; parfois elles s'adjoignent une grande collerette, également plis-

sée et sont taillées dans des shantungs légers ou des imprimés.

Le style de la collection atteint son apogée avec toute une série de robes de mousseline dont les jupes sont délicieusement nonchalantes.

Pour le soir, des deux-pièces à casaque droite fendue de côté comme les blouses siamoises, de longs fourreaux glissants, de grandes cloches boules enroulées en portefeuille, des robes courtes à jupes « dansantes » et petits corsages justaucorps. Certaines de ces robes ont un buste allongé, l'ampleur se montant sous la taille, cuirassés de pierreries, les corsages ont l'apparence d'une cote de mailles.

Après les avoir cherchés toute la journée, la femme, le soir, a retrouvé ses manches.

DIOR a dit "oui"

a liberté la femme

« R a dit « oui » : la berté de la femme nouvelle est donc certaine aussi. Il n'y a pas cette saison de silhouette X, Y, Z. Il n'y a de ligne-sac, de ligne-trapèze, de ligne-empire, que les couturiers suivent tous avec un bel accord.

...a un style 1959 qui veut ... épaules élargies, une taille naturelle, des jupes à un, deux ... trois centimètres du genou; ... évite les excès et les déguisements; et qui laisse un grand choix aux femmes.

... seule grande nouveauté ... retour au tailleur classique... ... l'avait déjà vu chez Nina ... on l'a revu chez Dior. Il ... partout l'hiver prochain.

DIOR :
...use de marin et ...eau mousquetaire

... Dior, cette saison, la ... vue par Yves Saint-Lau... ... est jeune, simple, très élé... ... très raffinée.

... surtout aimé la première ... de la collection. C'est au ... en effet, que reviennent ... mais tailleurs, les classi... ... coupés comme des vestons ... me et fleuris d'une bran... ... de muguet, d'un œillet, ... marguerite ou d'un camé...

... mi eux, de très jolis deux-pièces ressemblant aux vareuses ... marins, presque tou... ... bleu marine clair ; leur ... col s'ouvre en corbeille ... ... modestie de jersey ou ... ... onza blanc. Leur dos droit ... ule une fermeture ; leur ... ... légèrement appuyé, met ... ...leur taille et poitrine.

... sous, des robes jeunes, ... et charmantes : jupes ... ... plis plats, petits corsa... ... décolletés à la manière ... ... maillot de marin, et cein... ... de box de trois à quatre ... ... mètres.

... sus, des manteaux désin... ... et confortables : pardes... ... étroits et glissants, les ... ... pets » ou paletots trois... ... qui ont la forme et les ... ... anchures larges d'un ciré ... marin.

... robes du soir se sont, ... saison, considérablement ... és. Dior n'est plus le ... ... pion de la paillette et de ... ... broderie : cela rajeunit ... ... oup sa collection. Les ... robes de mousseline ... ... dansant au moindre pas: ... ... tes collerettes plates ou ... ... es, corsages souples, ou ... ... res-corselet, jupes aériens ... ... les femmes dans ces ... ... sont des « Botticelli ». ... plus jolie — Valentine — ... a mousseline rouge camé... ... ccompagnée d'une grande ... ... ne fleurie romantique. ... elle aussi.

... a mode Dior encore : les ... ...aux d'homme le plus élé... ... en paille turquoise, porté ... ... œil, est un vrai chapeau ... ... ousquetaire) ; les petits ... ...iers chers à Monet, en... ... de voilettes ; les cape... ... en même flanelle grise ... tailleur, mais doublés ... ... paille de couleur vive : ... ... par exemple ; les colliers ... ... de grosses boules de verre ... : bleu saphir, rouge gre... ... aune topaze, vert émerau... ... olet améthyste ; les grap... ... marguerites échevelées en ... ... de bois, de corne ; les ... ... simples boutons de cuir ... ... mandarine » qui mettent ... ...let chaud sur les jambes ... ... bas pour jeune mariée ... ...ostés de motifs en perle...

I see the end of an era in Paris

by

JOY MATTHEWS

PARIS, THURSDAY

THE House of Dior has raised the white flag. It has given up the gimmicks and the gunfire and settled down to design elegant, flattering, natural-looking clothes in the true French manner.

It is the first time that I have been to a Dior collection where women have not been asked to make themselves look like something else—magnets, tulips, bodkins, arrows, and trapezes.

All St. Laurent asks you to do is to look like a woman. He even calls his collection Silhouette Naturelle.

His line is "long," or so he says. But all that means is that your dress is straight and beautifully fitting, your skirt a little below the knee (about two to three inches) and that you stand up straight. Not much dictatorship there!

No, it looks as if the women have won.

Charming

MAYBE it wasn't a masterpiece of invention on the part of St. Laurent, but I like it. And so did most of the women there. Only the gimmick girls looked glum.

What everyone is asking, will this mean? Has St. Laurent lost the throne to another?

It means we are back to the pre-war days when you came to Paris to *see Paris clothes*: when you concentrated on being elegant and well dressed and not a sight for everyone to stare at.

It means that instead of one man hitting the high spot every six months with a new shape, there will be five or six different Paris couture houses that will sell to the world.

The Paris dress has returned, rather than the Dior copy. The roundabout has slowed down and there are more designers on the roundabout.

At this moment I would say there are St. Laurent, Cardin, La Roche, Patou, and one about to step on: Nina Ricci, who yesterday showed a very charming collection.

jumper suit with a wide V-neckline or a collar and a modesty vest.

The tops of these suits come nearly to the hips and the skirts are straight. My favourite was in navy blue wool, collarless, the V filled in with white ribbed cotton knitting which showed again about an inch from the sleeves.

With this was a small back-of-the-head hat that banded with white cotton knitting.

These jumpers and suits looked easy to wear and to copy.

The coats were rather mannish, often double-breasted and seven-eighths in length, with slim skirts showing beneath. Buttons were all tailored — bone or sometimes pearl. Sleeves were set in and very restrained. No marrows or balloon shapes here at all.

For cocktails there were some very simple black shantung sheath dresses, either with low, round necks or camisoled tops.

These buttoned in the front with man-tailored buttons, leaving the top button undone to show a small but alluring V just above the bosom. Typical Paris.

There were some fitted linen dresses for resort wear, sometimes embroidered, and with matching jackets. There was even an ankle-length evening dress in iris-blue linen.

Stop!

I DON'T know how the English wholesalers will feel about this collection, but I do know the American and French wholesalers will like it.

America has been trying to bring back the belts and the slim line for about six months now, and the French wholesalers asked St. Laurent recently if he would stop these terrific changes that were making life impossible for them.

The clothes themselves were pretty, but adult and elegant. Grey and navy blue were favourite colours for suits, coats, and day dresses.

There was a feeling of Savile-row, with a few rather tailored suits. Coats were definitely on the mannish side.

Perhaps St. Laurent ordered himself a few natty suitings in London—who knows?

My favourite

I SEE the slim, practical sheath dresses, belted in leather at the natural waist, with simple round neck and short sleeves, selling like mad.

Some were sleeveless, some were pleated, but they were all in tailored fabrics, flannels, worsteds, and smooth wools.

Over these were short easy jackets with small collars set well away from the neck and threequarter sleeves.

St. Laurent's answer to the jersey and skirt is a tailored

Pleats

DRESSY dresses were a bit too dressy for me. Chiffon was much in use again. Some dresses were pleated all over, including the wide collar which looked rather like the frill on Pierrot's tunic.

They looked a little too vicarage-garden-party for me. Any Englishwoman who dared to wear one of these at Ascot would be labelled a real frump.

Evening dresses were either short—that is, three inches below the knee — or ankle length. Prettiest of all was in a soft pink organza with a bell skirt coming to the ankle, caught in with a wide matching belt and three-quarter sleeves.

Rose-like

THERE were also some very expensive-looking dresses in finely pleated chiffon and rows and rows of Valenciennes lace in navy, white, or black, and one short evening dress was in red material with a simple draped bodice and the whole skirt made of huge rose-petals to give the look of a full-blown rose.

All in all, I preferred the morning and early evening dresses in this collection.

This is not a remarkably new collection, but you will want to wear it.

And it is a very important collection, for it marks the end of an era, the end of the ever-changing silhouette that dominated not only Paris but London too, for although London designers hated sacks and the trapeze, they did not dare to ignore them.

Now it remains to be seen if their collections, starting next week, will be as restrained and natural as the French have dared to be.

CUP FINAL CRUSH
(plus champagne)
AT DIOR'S

St. Laurent's Sailor Girl Deserves Praise

PARIS, Thursday.

IT was a happy **Yves St. Laurent** who responded with smiles and kisses to the resounding applause for his collection to-day. With **Mme. Zenacher** and **Mme. Marguerite** to left and right, cameras on all sides, and midinettes mingling with the crowds on the Avenue Montaigne calling for him outside, it was a fabulous morning.

He deserved his applause. Without a doubt, this young designer has proved himself worthy of his inheritance from **Christian Dior.**

To get out of Dior's was like trying to push one's way through a Cup Final crowd, and I became one of the casualties bathed in champagne.

Natural Line

Instead of a fancy name for his new collection St. Laurent states simply: "A natural silhouette and a long line."

Within this framework, the inspiration of his line is the sailor girl look—hip-length easy tunics with flattering cutaway collars over a vestee. Jackets with similar cutaway collars with narrow revers are worn over chic dresses with plain, square-cut necklines to allow the same "vestee" detail.

He has no hesitation about the hemline. He hates knees to show and has the longest skirts of the important designers. The new length is still young-looking, but discreet—two to three inches below the knee, depending on the mannequin's height.

For the sophisticated sailor girl his skirts are slim; for the *jeune fille* they are knife pleated.

To complete this theme, the young girl has a flyaway sailor hat; the sophisticated woman a small veiled boater or bowler.

After the sailor tunics come naturally - belted sheath dresses under jackets that

From Winefride Jackson

sometimes have not only décolleté collars but just half-fronts, revealing the full length of the dress.

St. Laurent has abandoned last season's very loose top in favour of a more tailored shoulder line, even reviving the classic tailor-made suit with set-in sleeves and semi-fitted waist. On the whole, though, shoulders and sleeves tend to be magyar cut, but more fitted.

Belts, belts, and more belts. They are used on wool dresses, on pleated chiffon shirt styles for afternoon, on bouffant button-through silks for cock-tails, and on embroidered long chiffons for evening.

Stoles Again

Another reprieve for that ubiquitous and hardy annual,

By an Englishman in Paris

*B*RIGHT *star of the Paris millinery world this season is a young Englishman, Graham Smith. He is designing hats for Lanvin-Castillo. Here is one of them, a turban in navy satin with a green rose.*

given a slight lift in front) were, I thought, the prettiest.

Colours: Navy with white trimmings, as becomes the sailor girl; rich peony red,

masterpiece of stage production to launch a new hat style was to use the same design throughout the collection. This was a boater with the

YES, DIOR'S 'HEIR' IS GOOD—BUT NOT YET GREAT

From AILSA GARLAND

Mirror Woman's Editor, Paris, Thursday.

TODAY, with the third collection shown by Yves St. Laurent, who succeeded to the great Dior fashion empire when Christian Dior died in 1957, it is possible to assess St. Laurent's work.

In my view he is GOOD . . . but NOT GREAT.

In any other fashion house St. Laurent might well be great. But it is hard for him, a twenty-two-year-old, to succeed to the throne of a man who was unique.

Certainly St. Laurent is not great enough to change a woman's shape in opposition to other designers as Dior himself so often did. St. Laurent makes becoming clothes in heavenly fabrics. They are the kind of clothes most women dream of owning.

But more is expected of the GREAT Paris salons.

They have to set a line that can be copied by ready-to-wear dress makers . . . a line so definite that even when it is adapted it still bears their signature.

Yves loses the hemline battle

YVES ST. LAURENT has lost the Battle of the Hemline. His attempt to bring back longer skirts has failed.

Last season St. Laurent dropped hemlines in opposition to the extremely short skirts of other designers.

Women did not want to wear longer hemlines.

And this season the St. Laurent hemline is SHORT. Like the hemlines which every other Paris designer has shown, it is an inch or two below the knee.

Dresses Like Bells

☆ St. Laurent's ideas vary only in detail from what I have been reporting every day since the shows started.

JACKETS are either short and semi-fitting or hip-length and belted.

Sleeveless OVERBLOUSES are worn to

After the show... a kiss for Mum

● Fashion designer Yves St. Laurent, whose newest creations were shown in Paris yesterday, is pictured above kissing his mother after receiving her congratulations.

INDIA TO INVITE QUEEN?

THE immense success of the Duke of Edinburgh's present tour of India has raised Indian hopes of a visit by the Queen, reports Reuter.

Informed observers in B o m b a y,— and these include d i p l o m a t s— believe that if everything goes smoothly during the Duke's forthcoming visit to Calcutta a FORMAL invitation may be sent to Buckingham Palace.

A special eye will be kept on Calcutta because, it is said, the vast, volatile crowds there make police control difficult.

In Bombay yesterday the Duke had a terrific reception. More than a million people came out to cheer him.

SCHOOLGIRLS PELTED HIM WITH ROSE PETALS AND JASMINE BUDS.

He visited the Indian atomic energy establishment at Trombay.

size cummerbund.

It is surely the broadest belt in Paris. One of these belts was in coral on a grey flannel sleeveless dress. Another was in scarlet on a navy dress.

The Prettiest

☆ St. Laurent showed more navy and black than the other designers. But the rest of his colours were the same as theirs . . coral, yellow, white and shades of red.

His short evening GOWNS, a galaxy of heavenly fabrics, had small shoulder straps or sleeves, but for ball gowns, of course, the bodices were strapless.

His two prettiest evening dresses were:

A shell p i n k silk, very simple, with a floor-length bell skirt and a high, wide sash: and

A white satin, the bodice completely covered with embroidery or coral beads.

☆ Designer C H A N E L, whose cardigan suit creations have swept the world t o d a y, showed one with a slightly shorter and oh-so-slightly m o r e fitted jacket than usual.

Her cardigan suits in soft pastel tweeds, navy and white, navy and red, or black and white, will continue to be winners.

DIOR sets

PARIS, Thursday

YVES ST. LAURENT, Dior's successor, has become every woman's boyfriend. To-day he revealed his new line for spring. It's the Freedom Line—and it's hit the jackpot.

The reason? He's given us back our figures again. Now it's normal for a woman to look like a woman again.

And so when his new styles were shown there came the old familiar, frenzied Dior roar and cry of " Bravo, Bravo."

Last season the cheers were a little muted. To-day they were enthusiastic.

The 23-year-old boy with the owl glasses and the draped-shaped suit is to-day the idol of Paris.

☆ At his show he gave us back our waists, and put them back where they belong—at the natural waist-line.

☆ He gave us back belts to mark that waist.

☆ And he clipped two inches off his last

EDNA McKENNA reports on YVES ST LAURENT

season's hemline to bring it in line with the other designers, who have dropped theirs by about the same.

So St. Laurent's hemline is about 14 inches from the ground, still an inch longer than the other French designers. It's a perfect compromise on both sides.

St. Laurent shows jackets with brief basques filled in by leather belts. He gives us dresses with slim sleeveless tops and slim skirts all marked at the waist by a belt.

But the waist is never pulled in and it never looks wasped.

When I congratulated

St. Laurent after the show I asked: "Don't you think it's a little soon to put belts back again at the natural waist?"

He hesitated, smiled and said: "I do not. It seems to me that this was just the perfect moment for such a decision."

He made the statement with so much more confidence than he would a year ago.

ST. LAURENT HAS PROVED HIMSELF THE APOSTLE OF COMPROMISE.

For women not yet ready to go back to fitted waists he provides an equally important loose-fitting line that is unbelted and easy fitting.

Middies

He demonstrates this line with three types of jumper tops.

1 Brief waistcoats that end at the waist.

2 Middy blouses that slither over the hips and finish half-way down the hip.

3 Very loose-fitting coolie jackets slit down the front and reaching to mid-thigh.

For evening he carries on this line in shimmering gauzes and lamé. There is a strong nautical feeling about the whole collection.

Slim hips

Collars are shoulder-wide and have small revers. They are filled in with modesty vests. If the models never turned around you would have

left the show i there was a sail at the back.

The hips are unemphasised. the skirt just lifts hips and eases down to a narrow

Instead of s Laurent provides over belted dre loose jerkins. In could count the true suits on the one hand.

Teenag

There are few He prefers thre coats usually be matching dresse

The coats are and the necklin in with a foula often sprinkled w dots.

Every young g be happy that St has two teenag They have in whole series of afternoon dress pleated bertha little waists and blown skirts that flounced.

These might taken for con dresses except are in pretty pa

Charm

There's an exc ankle-length for dresses. It has flavour, for the out over the hips curves in towards

St. Laurent's real charmers.

Straw coolies ripe cherries, lil valley or filled f bucket-shaped c printed fabrics . . " little boy blue " tiny turned-back

☆ High-style fur coats like this are in every shop in Paris. This, from king of fashion Balenciaga, features the Empire Line. The fur is guanaco— a large, wild llama of the Andes.

Whoosh! The dish are do

THIS has been a good week for the housewife — there's been a spate of new ideas and developments to make life easier

For instance, I've seen a compact dishwashing machine that will fit on a draining board (and under it when not in use). It works on a turbine principle from water pressure, so it doesn't add to your gas or electricity bills.

For parties

Just connect it to the sink tap—and your dishes, glasses and cutlery are clean in a minute. Cost: 32 guineas, but it's obtainable on HP.

For party fare, or giving your main meal a special look, hot or cold, there are some seasoned puffed potato slices—1s. a bag.

NOW there's the

packaged kitche ment—you ca your kitchen, the pieces toge out screwdrive mer, nails or minutes.

It's a Scan idea brought h month and corner, tall an cupboards, boards and sink everything the n ticular of ho could want in kitchen.

FURNISHING make news, to derful for curt the extensive 5ft. wide cot Finnish designe Sarpaneva.

They save because of the width. The cost 21s. a yard

JOAN D

hat I liked best ...hed on the top ...d like a pin ...d was stuck all ... white flowers ... could have black hat-pins.

...ent is my very ...ourite, too. I ...g myself that it ... he shows so ...in his collection.

...ue, washed-out ...hyacinth blue ...s of prints that ...s mixed with ...ns or black.

...y replaces black ...much less black

than in a normal Dior collection—but plenty of spring and summer colours, including all the pinks, salmon, blush, roses and shell.

Dig deep into your trinket box and bring out all the beads you can collect. Wear them this spring with one of the new wider necklines.

St. Laurent shows great masses of beads—pearls mixed with crystals, blue crystals were mixed with pearls on a navy dress and the vast straw hat was in the identical same shade of pale blue.

Le secret des plus jolies robes de Dior

★ La collection Dior a été conçue en quinze jours par Yves-Mathieu Saint-Laurent : elle se composait de mille dessins, elle a donné naissance à cent quatre-vingt-cinq modèles, réalisés en un mois et demi par huit cents ouvrières.

Si Mme Onassis ou Mme Boussac décidaient d'acheter la totalité de la collection, il leur en coûterait quatre-vingt-deux millions...

★ « Hula hoop », robe vedette de Yves-Mathieu Saint-Laurent, a failli ne pas être présentée dans la collection. Le matin même, à 8 heures, une « première » attendait sur le quai de la gare de l'Est l'arrivée des broderies venant de Saint-Quentin, indispensables aux parements de la robe. La robe a été achevée un quart d'heure avant sa présentation.

★ « Pourquoi êtes-vous devenu couturier ? », demandait-on à Yves-Mathieu Saint-Laurent.

« J'ai eu deux grandes rencontres dans ma vie : les poupées de ma sœur, que j'ai habillées à 9 ans ; j'y ai pris goût et, dix ans plus tard, Christian Dior m'a offert d'habiller ses mannequins. Je dois avouer que j'ai gardé une secrète préférence pour les poupées de ma sœur... »

★ On demandait à Yves-Mathieu Saint-Laurent :

— Que pensez-vous des femmes, vous qui les habillez et les voyez, pour ainsi dire, sans apprêt ?

— Elles sont très décevantes. Heureusement qu'on les habille. Sinon, personne ne s'intéresserait (peut-être) à elles...

★ — A quel moment êtes-vous devenu un homme ? Quel est l'événement qui a décidé de votre évolution de caractère ?

— Je n'ai pas l'intention, dit Yves-Mathieu Saint-Laurent, de devenir un homme. Dieu merci ! je reste un enfant, il n'y a pas de

moments importants dans ma vie ; je joue...

★ Les quatre plus jolies robes de la collection Dior, selon Yves-Mathieu Saint-Laurent, ont été inventées pour ses meilleures amies : pour Eglantine, sa chienne, une robe du soir rose ; pour Zouzou, le petit basset de sa jeunesse, robe grise d'après-midi,

assez stricte ; pour Hazel, un chihuahua, petite chienne de son ami Pierre Bergé, robe d'après-midi plissée noire ; pour Valentine, la fille de Zizi Jeanmaire, robe du soir rouge avec grande collerette.

★ Yves-Mathieu Saint-Laurent a, depuis son enfance, un violon d'Ingres. Il s'est constitué un petit théâtre en carton sur lequel il interprète, avec des petits personnages découpés et habillés par lui, les classiques. Sa pièce favorite est « L'Ecole des femmes », dans le décor du regretté Bébé Bérard.

Biography

1936 – August 1st: Yves Henri Donat Mathieu-Saint-Laurent is born at the Jarsaillon clinic, Oran (Algeria). The son of Lucienne Wilbaux and Charles Mathieu-Saint-Laurent, he will become the eldest of three children in the family home at 11 rue Stora.

1942 – September: He is enrolled in a Catholic school: "At the age of 6, I became someone else."

1948 – September: He begins attending the college of the Sacred Heart. He makes his first dresses out of paper for the dolls in his Illustrious Theatre and gives performances for his sisters. It marks the birth of a passion for Jean Cocteau's *Two-headed Eagle* and Scarlett O'Hara in *Gone with the Wind*.

1949 – February 23rd: He starts to edit *Pourquoi parler d'amour?* (*Why speak of love?*). His first dress designs for his mother and sisters are made by a seamstress. The designs are inspired by Jean-Gabriel Domergue.

1950 – May 9th: He attends a performance of Molière's *School for Women* at Oran's Municipal Theatre. The play is produced by Jouvet, who also plays the role of Arnolphe. The sets are designed by Christian Bérard. Yves undertakes a variety of theatre projects, and sketches in the style of Bérard, Gruau, Dior, Balenciaga, and Givenchy. He recopies and illustrates *Les Caprices de Marianne* by Musset, and *Madame Bovary* by Flaubert in watercolors.

1951 – Summer: Yves creates the "cave de jazz" in the family home in Trouville (Oran) and throws existentialist parties.

1952 – June: Yves gets his first press review. In the *Echo d'Oran*, an unknown journalist hails the "magnificent costumes designed by the 15-year-old Yves Mathieu-Saint-Laurent" for the Children's Gala at the Municipal Opera.

1954 – February: Yves starts to write to Michel de Brunhoff. The correspondence will continue until February 1955. Alongside the letters, Yves also sends some of his theatre and fashion sketches.
June: Yves takes his baccalaureate at the lycée Lamoricière.
September: Enrolled by his father at the Federation of Haute Couture, Yves moves to Paris. However, he only stays with the federation a mere three months. Yves meets Fernando Sanchez, who will remain one of his closest friends.
November 25th: Yves wins first and third prize in the "dress" category at the Wool Secretariat Competition. The model, a black crêpe cocktail dress, will ultimately be made in the studios of Hubert de Givenchy.
December: Yves receives his prize at Maxim's. (The first prize in the "coats" category is awarded to Karl Lagerfeld). He presents fifty new sketches to Michel de Brunhoff. Brunhoff in turn shows them to his friend Christian Dior.

1955 – June 20th: Yves Mathieu-Saint-Laurent is hired at Dior as an assistant designer in the studio. First dress, first photo: *Dovima and the elephants* (Avedon), 1955.

1956 – Yves is introduced to Paris society at Baron de Rédé's "bal de têtes" at the Hotel Lambert. He meets Zizi Jeanmaire and Roland Petit.

1957 – October 24th: Christian Dior dies of a heart attack in Montecatini (Italy) at the age of 52.
November 15th: Yves Mathieu-Saint-Laurent is named to replace Christian Dior. He becomes Yves Saint Laurent. At 21, he is the youngest couturier in the world.

1958 – January 30th: Yves shows his first collection and triumphs with the "Trapeze" line. It earns him the Neiman Marcus Award. He is nicknamed "Christian II" and "the forlorn young man."
February 3rd: Yves meets Pierre Bergé for the second time. Their first meeting had taken place a few days earlier when Bergé came to congratulate him after the fashion show. Pierre Bergé, who was born on the île d'Oléron in 1930, arrived in Paris in 1948, and managed the ascending career of the painter Bernard Buffet.

1960 – January 1958 to July 1960: Yves creates six collections for Dior. He shows the first black leather jackets for couture (in crocodile). The Chanel influence: "The line loses itself to the benefit of a style" (Natural Line, Summer 1959). The goyescas and the infantes.
September: Yves Saint Laurent is called up to serve his country. He is replaced at Dior by Marc Bohan.
October/November: He spends six weeks in the Val-de-Grâce military hospital for nervous depression.
He is discharged on November 14th. Pierre Bergé celebrates his thirtieth birthday. They leave for the Canary Islands.

1961 – January: The beginning of a life spent together with Pierre Bergé. Yves files suit against the House of Dior for breach of contract.
July: In association with Pierre Bergé, Yves decides to open his own couture house. Three former colleagues from Dior follow him: They are the model Victoire, who is named salon director, Claude Licard, and Gabrielle Buchaert.
November 14th: Yves signs a contract with Atlanta businessman J. Mack Robinson, the first American to invest in a Parisian couture house. His name will not be made public until 1963.
December: The first dress, labelled 0001, is made for Mrs. Arturo Lopez Willshaw. Yves designs the costumes (the "thing with feathers," the little black pullover) for Zizi Jeanmaire for her show at the Alhambra, and for *The Itinerants*, a piece choreographed by Roland Petit. The graphic designer Cassandre creates the YSL logo. Yves moves his studios to the former townhouse of the painter Forain at 30 bis, rue Spontini (Paris, 16th arrondissement).
Half of his new workers come from Dior.
December 4th: The official opening of the House of Saint Laurent.

1962 – January 29th: Yves Saint Laurent presents his first house collection: "The best array of suits since Chanel" (*Life*). The "Now Look," and the "foundations" of the Saint Laurent style: the blouse, the *caban* (sailor's jacket), the smock, the coat. "Yves Saint Laurent's greatest talent is to give an aristocratic allure to the whimsies of his time" (Lucien François, *Combat*, February 23rd 1962).

1963 – April: Yves makes his first trip to Japan, and signs a contract with Seibu. His collection is presented in Osaka and Tokyo. Mishima's *School of Flesh*, published the same year, evokes the child "with nerves of steel."

1964 – Launch of the perfume *Y*.

1965 – July: Yves' "Mondrian" collection triumphs (haute couture, winter 1965). "The best collection" according to the *New York Times*. For *Women's Wear Daily*, Yves Saint Laurent becomes "the King of Paris": "I was tired of making dresses for blasé millionairesses." Yves makes his first trip to New York. The house is sold to Richard Salomon (Charles of the Ritz). The period also marks the beginning of a long friendship with Rudolf Nureyev and Margot Fonteyn, whom he dresses both on stage and for the city. Costumes for *Notre-Dame de Paris*. (Roland Petit, TNP).

1966 – January: Yves presents his first smoking suit (haute couture, summer 1966). It will henceforth become a "signature" of the creator appearing in each of his collections. The same year, he presents his first transparencies: The "nude look."
July: The "Pop Art" collection (haute couture, winter 1966). Yves meets Andy Warhol.
September 26th: The very first Rive Gauche boutique opens at 21, rue de Tournon (Paris, 6th arrondissement). The boutique is christened by Catherine Deneuve. It is Yves Saint Laurent who designs the costumes for her in *Belle de Jour*, a film based on the novel by Joseph Kessel and adapted for the screen by Luis Buñuel.

1967 – January: Yves unveils his Bambara dresses, a collection inspired by tribal African art (haute couture, summer 1967).
Yves' comic strip, *La Vilaine Lulu* (Naughty Lulu) is published (by Tchou Editions). It is the culmination of a project that first began when he started working at Dior in 1955.

The same year, Yves Saint Laurent discovers Marrakech. He and Pierre Bergé buy "the snake house," a villa in the city's Medina district. He also meets Loulou de la Falaise and Thalita Getty, the Gypsy billionaire.

1968 – January: Yves presents the *saharienne*, the first safari jacket: The "Safari Look." The first jumpsuit; the dawn of black and costume jewelry. The Smoking-bermuda and the cigaline see-through blouse. "I suddenly became aware of the female form. I started to have a dialogue with women and to understand what a modern woman was." Betty Catroux, a close friend. The "II" style.
February 11th: Gabrielle Chanel designates Yves as her spiritual heir on the TV program "Dim Dam Dom": "Someday, someone will have to carry on my work."
September: The first Yves Saint Laurent Rive Gauche boutique opens in New York.
"Yves' name is magic" (*Time*, September 27th 1968). "When it's pants, it's Yves" (Lauren Bacall). The dawn of the evening mini dress and his first menswear-inspired suits. The influence of Marlene Dietrich.

1969 – The first Rive Gauche boutique for men opens.

1971 – January 10th: Gabrielle Chanel dies at the age of 78. Three weeks later, Yves Saint Laurent presents his "Liberation" collection. The new retro style causes a scandal. Calling haute couture an "old lady" he announces his desire to renounce it. The launch of *Rive Gauche*, "not a perfume for the self-effacing women." He poses nude (photo, Jeanloup Sieff) to promote his first eau de toilette for men: "I'm ready to do anything to sell myself." Costumes for the Casino de Paris: Zizi, the dancer Jorge Lago, and the costumes for the "Proust" ball at the château de Ferrières (December 2nd).

1972 – Yves Saint Laurent and Pierre Bergé buy the couture house and develop licensing contracts. They also build a significant collection of Impressionist and Modern art and amass a collection of 1930s furniture.
Warhol creates a series of portraits of Yves Saint Laurent. Loulou enters the studio and becomes the muse.
"Yves Saint Laurent has changed the face of fashion and perhaps its future," writes Nina Hyde in the *Washington Post*. March 24th: Cristobal Balenciaga dies at the age of 77.

1973 – November 13th: Elsa Schiaparelli dies at the age of 83.

1974 – July 14th: Yves moves the fashion house to a Napoleon III-era townhouse at 5 Avenue Marceau (Paris, 16th arrondissement). In Marrakech, Pierre Bergé and Yves Saint Laurent buy the "house of serene happiness."

1975 – Yves launches his androgynous style: The "Lean Look" and the black lines are at their apogee. The year also sees the launch of the perfume *Eau libre*.

1976 – July: Yves presents his "Opéra-Ballets russes" collection (haute couture, winter 1976). "I don't know if it's the best but it's certainly the most beautiful" he says. The collection is an international success earning him unprecedented front-page coverage in the *New York Times*: "A revolutionary collection which will change t he course of fashion in the world" (Bernadine Morris). "It's not a nostalgia for the past, but the eternal present, which is on the other side of the past," writes Pierre Schneider (*Vogue* USA).

1978 – March 1977/1978: The red and the pink. The imaginary voyages. The great collections on the theme of exoticism: The Spain of Velasquez, the Morocco of Delacroix, and China with the launch of Opium perfume October 12th 1977. On September 16th 1977, Maria Callas dies. For Yves, it is "the end of a dream." He writes a tribute to her that will be published in *Le Monde* two days later.

1979 – July: A tribute to Picasso, Aragon, Apollinaire ("tout terriblement"), Cocteau ("The shattered mirror"), the "Shakespeare" collection (haute couture, winter 1979).

1980 – In Marrakech, Pierre Bergé and Yves Saint Laurent buy the Majorelle Gardens and the Villa Oasis, previously owned by Majorelle.

1981 – Creation of a uniform for Marguerite Yourcenar, the first woman ever to be admitted to the Académie Française. The tribute to Matisse.

1982 – January 29th: Yves celebrates the 20th anniversary of the House of Saint Laurent at the Lido, where he receives the International Fashion Award from the Council of Fashion Designers of America.

1983 – January: The pink and black collection and the launch of the perfume *Paris*. Pierre Bergé and Yves Saint Laurent buy Château Gabriel in Benerville-sur-Mer (Normandy). It is the same château when Proust met the publisher Gallimard.
December 5th: Launch of the perfume *Paris*. Inauguration of the exhibition "Yves Saint Laurent, 25 years of creation" at the Metropolitan Museum of Art in New York.
The brainchild of Diana Vreeland, it is the largest retrospective ever devoted to a living couturier (1 million visitors). Yves Saint Laurent's name enters the Larousse dictionary.

1985 – March 12th: At the Élysée Palace, French President François Mitterrand makes Yves a knight of the Légion d'honneur.
May 6th: Yves makes his first visit to China for an exhibition that has been devoted to his works at the Beijing Gallery of Fine Arts.
October 23rd: To honor him for lifetime achievement, Yves receives the "Fashion Oscar" for greatest couturier at the Opéra de Paris.

1986 – May: An exhibition of his works opens at the Musée des Arts de la Mode.
November: Yves Saint Laurent and Pierre Bergé buy back the Saint Laurent perfumes, thus creating the Yves Saint Laurent group.

1987 – Yves Saint Laurent exhibitions are staged in Moscow (The House of Artists and Writers), Leningrad (The Hermitage), and Sydney. Andy Warhol dies on February 22nd.
October: Yves Saint Laurent pays tribute to David Hockney in his Rive Gauche collection.

1988 – January: With embroidery inspired by Van Gogh's *Sunflowers* and *Irises*, Yves presents the most expensive jackets in the world. The tribute to Cubism. "To give motion to that which is static on the body of a woman" (*Paris Match*, February 1988).
September 9th: Yves Saint Laurent becomes the first couturier to present his creations at the Fête de l'Humanité, a festival organised by the French Communist Party.

1990 – January: The "Tributes" collection (Bernard Buffet, Zizi Jeanmaire, Marcel Proust, Catherine Deneuve…).

1991 – January: Pierre Bergé tells the *Nouvel Observateur* that "Haute Couture is doomed" (January 24th).

1992 – January 29th: Yves Saint Laurent presents "Renaissance," his 121st collection: With a palette based on Matisse's Morocco period it includes the "bubble" shapes of his first collection (January 1958).
February 3rd: 2, 800 guests celebrate 30 years of the house of Yves Saint Laurent at the Bastille Opera.

1993 – January 19th: The Yves Saint Laurent Group is sold to Sanofi. Yves Saint Laurent and Pierre Bergé retain control of the haute couture operations.
May 17th: The buyout is approved by the stockholders of the two companies at their annual general meeting. With the acquisition of Yves Saint Laurent, Sanofi becomes the third largest luxury fragrance and cosmetics group in the world after l'Oréal and Estée Lauder.
July 2nd: Pierre Bergé is named UNESCO's Goodwill Ambassador.
Le Monde journalist Laurence Benaïm writes the first biography of Yves Saint Laurent (Grasset, Paris).

1995 – January 1st: Yves Saint Laurent is promoted to the rank of officer of the Légion d'honneur.

1997 – September 26th: After paying tribute to Russia in his celebrated "Opéra Ballets russes" haute couture collection in 1976, Yves Saint Laurent opens his first boutique in Moscow. His winter 1997-1998 haute couture collection is dedicated to the women of the Renaissance. "Black is the color of Renaissance portraits; of Clouet, Agnès Sorel, and the Valois court of Frans Hals."

1998 – March: The International Fashion Photography Festival stages an exhibition of over eighty images of the creations of Yves Saint Laurent, as seen by fashion photographers. The exhibition will ultimately travel to Berlin, Sydney, Tokyo, and Paris.
On July 12th, just moments before the kick-off of the World Cup soccer final, a fashion show with three hundred models is staged at the Stade de France arena. The show is seen by two billion viewers worldwide.

1999 – January: creation of the association for the promotion of the works of Yves Saint Laurent.
A center at La Villette (Paris) opens with over 4,000 of Yves Saint Laurent's creations. The items include the most important models since 1958 and a variety of accessories (jewelry, scarves, belts, shoes, hats). The center is open by appointment to journalists, students and fashion professionals. In addition, it regroups all the sketches that Yves Saint Laurent made for the theatre and music hall—over 400 in all.
June 2nd: Yves Saint Laurent receives the New York Fashion Council's Designers of America Lifetime Achievement Award in New York.

2000 – Elf Sanofi sells the Yves Saint Laurent group to Gucci. Yves Saint Laurent and Pierre Bergé retain control of Yves Saint Laurent haute couture.

2001 – March 24th: Yves Saint Laurent receives the Palerme la Rosa d'Oro. The prize is in recognition of his lifetime achievements and the impact of his work on modern culture.
July 14th: Yves Saint Laurent is promoted to the rank of Commander of the Order of the Légion d'honneur by Jacques Chirac, President of the French Republic.

2002 – January 23rd: Yves Saint Laurent celebrates forty years of his couture house.

Theatre

1959

CYRANO DE BERGERAC
Choreographed by Roland Petit
Based on the novel by Edmond Rostand
Music by Marius Constant
Costumes by Yves Saint Laurent
Théâtre de l'Alhambra, Paris

1961

LES FORAINS
Choreographed by Roland Petit
Synopsis by Boris Kochno
Music by Henri Sauguet
For French Television

ZIZI JEANMAIRE SHOW
Produced by Roland Petit
Sets and costumes by
Yves Saint Laurent
Théâtre de l'Alhambra, Paris

1962

LES CHANTS DE MALDOROR
Choreographed by Roland Petit
Based on the work by Lautréamont
Music by Marius Constant
Sets and costumes by
Yves Saint Laurent
Théâtre national populaire, Paris

RHAPSODIE ESPAGNOLE
Choreographed by Roland Petit
Music by Maurice Ravel
Sets and costumes by
Yves Saint Laurent
Théâtre national populaire, Paris

1963

ZIZI JEANMAIRE SHOW
Produced by Roland Petit
Sets and costumes by
Yves Saint Laurent
Théâtre national populaire, Paris

1964

THE MARRIAGE OF FIGARO
Beaumarchais
Produced by Jean-Louis Barrault
Costumes by Yves Saint Laurent
Compagnie Renaud-Barrault
Odéon Théâtre de France, Paris

IL FAUT PASSER PAR LES NUAGES
François Billetdoux
Produced by Jean-Louis Barrault
Costumes by Yves Saint Laurent
Compagnie Renaud-Barrault
Odéon Théâtre de France, Paris

1965

ADAGE ET VARIATIONS
Choreographed by Roland Petit
Music by Francis Poulenc
Costumes by Yves Saint Laurent
Opéra national de Paris

NOTRE-DAME DE PARIS
Choreography by Roland Petit
Based on the novel by Victor Hugo
Music by Maurice Jarre
Costumes by Yves Saint Laurent
Opéra national de Paris

**DES JOURNÉES ENTIÈRES
DANS LES ARBRES**
Marguerite Duras
Costumes by Yves Saint Laurent
Compagnie Renaud-Barrault
Odéon Théâtre de France, Paris

1966

LES MONSTRES SACRÉS
Jean Cocteau
Costumes for Arletty
by Yves Saint Laurent
Théâtre des Ambassadeurs, Paris

1967

DELICATE BALANCE
Edward Albee
Costumes by Yves Saint Laurent
Compagnie Renaud-Barrault
Odéon Théâtre de France, Paris

1968

L'AMANTE ANGLAISE
Marguerite Duras
Produced by Claude Régy
Costumes for Madeleine Renaud
by Yves Saint Laurent
Théâtre national populaire, Paris
Salle Gémier

ZIZI JEANMAIRE SHOW
Produced by Roland Petit
Costumes by Yves Saint Laurent
Théâtre de l'Olympia, Paris

1970

ZIZI JEANMAIRE REVUE
Produced by Roland Petit
Sets and costumes by
Yves Saint Laurent
Casino de Paris

1972

REVUE ZIZI JEANMAIRE
Produced by Roland Petit
Sets and costumes by
Yves Saint Laurent
Casino de Paris

1973

LA ROSE MALADE
Choreographed by Roland Petit
Music by Gustav Mahler
Palais des Sports, Paris

HAROLD AND MAUDE
Colin Higgins
Produced by Jean-Louis Barrault
Costumes for Madeleine Renaud
by Yves Saint Laurent
Compagnie Renaud-Barrault
Théâtre Récamier, Paris

**LA CHEVAUCHEE
SUR LE LAC DE CONSTANCE**
Peter Handke

Produced by Claude Régy
Costumes by Yves Saint Laurent
Espace Cardin, Paris

SHÉHÉRAZADE
Choreographed by Roland Petit
Music by Maurice Ravel
Costumes by Yves Saint Laurent
Opéra national de Paris

1977

ZIZI JEANMAIRE REVUE
Produced by Roland Petit
Costumes by Yves Saint Laurent
Théâtre Bobino, Paris

1978

L'AIGLE À DEUX TETES
Jean Cocteau
Sets and costumes by
Yves Saint Laurent
Théâtre de l'Athénée Louis Jouvet,
Paris

INGRID CAVEN SHOW
Costumes for Ingrid Caven
by Yves Saint Laurent
Le Pigall's Cabaret, Paris

1980

CHER MENTEUR
Jérôme Kilty
Adaptation of Jean Cocteau's work
Sets and costumes by
Yves Saint Laurent
Théâtre de l'Athénée Louis Jouvet,
Paris

WINGS
Arthur Kopit
Adaptation of Matthieu Galey's work
Produced by Claude Régy
Costumes by Yves Saint Laurent
Théâtre d'Orsay, Paris

1983

SAVANNAH BAY
Marguerite Duras

Produced by Marguerite Duras
Costumes by Yves Saint Laurent
Théâtre du Rond-Point, Paris

2000

INGRID CAVEN SHOW
Costumes for Ingrid Caven
by Yves Saint Laurent
Odéon Théâtre de l'Europe, Paris

2001

VOYAGE D'HIVER
Costumes for Jessye Norman
by Yves Saint Laurent
Théâtre du Châtelet, Paris

Films

1960

LES COLLANTS NOIRS
Film by Terence Young
Costumes for Moira Shearer
by Yves Saint Laurent
Choreographed by Roland Petit

1963

THE PINK PANTHER
Film by Blake Edwards
Costumes for Claudia Cardinale
by Yves Saint Laurent

1965

ARABESQUE
Film by Stanley Donen
Costumes for Sophia Loren
by Yves Saint Laurent

1967

BELLE DE JOUR
Film by Luis Buñuel
Costumes for Catherine Deneuve
by Yves Saint Laurent

1968

LA CHAMADE
Film by Alain Cavalier
Based on the novel by Françoise Sagan
Costumes for Catherine Deneuve
by Yves Saint Laurent

1969

LA SIRÈNE DU MISSISSIPPI
Film by François Truffaut
Costumes for Catherine Deneuve
by Yves Saint Laurent

1974

STAVISKY
Film by Alain Resnais
Costumes for Anny Duperey
by Yves Saint Laurent

1975

UNE ANGLAISE ROMANTIQUE
Film by Joseph Losey
Costumes for Helmut Berger
by Yves Saint Laurent

1976

PROVIDENCE
Film by Alain Resnais
Costumes for Ellen Burstyn
by Yves Saint Laurent

Captions

1 – Yves Mathieu-Saint-Laurent's first few months, together with his parents.

2 – The swing in the family's garden at the Trouville house, a few miles from Oran, Algeria.

3 – The family in Oran during a Sunday meal.

4 – The Mathieu-Saint-Laurent villa in Trouville. This is where Yves Mathieu-Saint-Laurent spent the best moments of his childhood.

5 – Yves Mathieu-Saint-Laurent at age five.

6 – Yves Mathieu-Saint-Laurent at his first communion.

7 – The Mathieu-Saint-Laurent villa in Trouville.

8 – Lucienne Mathieu-Saint-Laurent with her children in her Trouville home. Michèle (born in 1942), Brigitte (born in 1945) and Yves, the oldest son, at age 11. In the middle, Bobinette, the dog.

9 - Yves Mathieu-Saint-Laurent at fifteen, in the garden with his friends.

10 – Yves Mathieu-Saint-Laurent amidst his theatre of model-dolls, made from the fabric of his mother's dresses.

11 – Yves Mathieu-Saint-Laurent at 18, before leaving Oran for Paris.

12 – Yves Mathieu-Saint-Laurent, first prize in «dresses» in the Wool Secretariat in 1954.

The design, a black crepe cocktail dress, would be made by Hubert de Givenchy.

13 – Yves Mathieu-Saint-Laurent, an assistant at Dior, in 1955.

14 – The Yves Saint Laurent Studio on Rue Spontini (16th Arrondissement, Paris), in the early 1970s. At his side is Anne-Marie Muñoz, his longtime collaborator.

15 – The Villa Oasis, built by the architect Majorelle in Marrakech, a city of inspiration for the designer and one of his vacation spots.

16 – The façade of the first Yves Saint Laurent couture house, Rue Spontini (16th Arrondissement, Paris).

17 – Yves Saint Laurent's office in the studio of his couture house, at 5 Avenue Marceau (16th Arrondissement, Paris).

Quotations

Genius is childhood rediscovered.

Fashions pass, style is eternal.
Fashion is futile, style is not.

Don't burn your wings at fashion's flame.

Fashion's poison kills.
Style enriches, develops, fortifies.

Women who follow fashion too closely run a great risk.
That of losing their profound nature, their style,
and their natural elegance.

Anyone can whimsically create a fashion.
Few can make a real piece of clothing.

Haute couture is a multitude of whispered secrets.
Those who have the privilege of transmitting them
are rare.

All creation is just re-creation, a new way of seeing
the same things, and expressing them differently,
specifying them, privileging one hitherto unnoticed
corner, or revealing their outlines.

To work on my dresses, to construct them, I need a
living model. A moving body. I couldn't work just on a
wooden mannequin. Because for me a piece of clothing
must move, and to then place it in everyday life I need
the presence of a woman's body.
Black models are privileged to have particularly
modern proportions and gestures. They adapt perfectly
to what I want, and I must say that they have always
brought me an enormous amount. I like the light they
give fabrics.
I think that the depth of their skin color brings out
the intensity of the colors better. They have never let
me down. I like their expressions, their bearing,
the way their eyes shine, their long lines, and the
irreversible suppleness of the way they walk. I feel they

have what is most magical about a woman. Mystery.
Not the old mystery of the *femmes fatales*, but
the dynamic mystery of a woman of today.

On pants
Since 1966, when the 1st tuxedo made its appearance
in my collection, the idea of a woman in a man's suit
has never stopped growing, deepening, imposing itself
as the very mark of a woman of today. I think that if
someday someone wanted to show a '70s woman, it
would have to be a woman in pants, because since '68,
pants have been one of the key pieces of a modern
woman's wardrobe.

A woman in a pant suit is not masculine at all—a severe
and implacable cut only emphasizes her femininity,
her seductiveness all the more. She comes to resemble
the body of an adolescent, that is, she affirms the great
revolution in manners that necessarily tends toward
uniformity and the equality of the sexes. This
androgynous woman, rendered equal to men by her
clothes, overturns the traditional image of classical
and outmoded femininity, deploying all those secret
weapons that are hers alone, especially makeup and
hairstyles, finally overcoming what could seem to be
a handicap, but what is in reality just the mysterious
and seductive image of today's woman.
P.S. A parallel to the affirmation of trousers, pant suits,
and blazers is the huge phenomenon of young women
in blue jeans.

My childhood refuses to die. It continues in me like
a secret.

Any work is good insofar as it expresses the man
who made it.

There are cheaters who use a power whose source
is outside them.

The light emanating from a being who loves is unlike
anything else.

Only Love preserves a being's beauty.

Love is the best cure for aging.

Love gives you wings that life undertakes to clip.

The best victories are those over oneself.

———————————————

Nothing is more beautiful than a naked body.
The most beautiful garment a woman can wear are
the arms of the man she loves.
But I am there for those who have not had the good
luck to find that happiness.

Fashion is a party.
To dress is to prepare to play a part.
A woman only becomes moving at the moment when
she cheats and Artifice comes into play.
I am not a couturier,
I am an artisan,
a manufacturer of happiness.

Every 25 years a body changes; the gestures, the
attitudes change.
There is a new body emerging slim and long and this
body is more important than any revolution dictated
by any designer.
The drama for luxury is that there are so many stupid
rich people. Luxury, so few know how to use it and
make it respectable.

When you feel good in a piece of clothing anything can
happen. A good outfit is a passport for happiness.

It's passé to speak of Revolution in fashion.
The true Revolution is elsewhere. The revolution
of the spirit will dictate the revolution of fashion.

———————————————

Youth

Youth is egotistical.
To grow older is to begin to think of others.

Youth is an illness that people often recover from
very late. In fact, some never do, and die of it.

The unease of aging comes from not having found
oneself.

———————————————

One may feel ashamed of one's happiness. Never
of one's suffering.
Joy and happiness can be mirages that hide from us
the reality of things and beings.
Serenity is the youth of the old.
It is without a doubt as beautiful as true youth.
It is a luxury anyone can afford, the culmination
of a life and its consecration. It is the opposite
of a privilege.
The only morality possible from one end of man's
existence to the other is Art, through which he can
hope to approach Happiness.

I think there is only one happiness possible on earth.
That of self-forgetting and devoting oneself to others.
When you try to make others happy, you eventually
receive a few flashes yourself.

———————————————

Elegance is a way of moving. It is also knowing how
to adapt to all of life's circumstances. Without the
elegance of the Heart, there is no elegance.

January 8, 1986
I am, as they say, a dog person. That is, I live with him
completely. Night and day. When I travel, I take him
with me, and when I can't, to England, for example,
I stay home. Lili Brik — who lived with Mayakovsky and
influenced him considerably — named him Moujik.
Lili later died, but Moujik is alive and well. We both
have our habits and our idiosyncrasies. Mainly,
though, I think we have the same tastes. That's
important. There are fabrics he loves — don't laugh —
the sound of taffeta when we unroll it drives him wild.
He has even been down a runway in a collection,
accompanying a suit as black and white as him.
So when my friend, Pierre Bergé, gave me Andy
Warhol's portrait of him last Christmas, I was
overwhelmed by joy and emotion. It was Moujik,
but it was also Andy, who painted my own portrait
more than fifteen years ago. Ever since then, although

Andy and didn't see each other often, I knew all about him, his career and his body of work, and I've always admired him. Alright, let's take the plunge and just say it: Moujik by Andy is the best Christmas present I could have ever hoped for.

"It is sometimes wisdom to be mad." (Cocteau) But fantasy may be tender, delicate, and poetic, or barbaric and savage. I broke all the rules, capturing the soul of the street, of daily events. I communicate my phantasms, I adapt them to my trade, but most of all I make them accessible to a woman's body.

Sometimes, I experience a great struggle within me between these phantasms and this woman's body — my rule being that I respect it. The body of Woman always triumphs, always wins, and I retreat behind her to avoid betraying the truth of my trade, my deepest truth, which is how much the reality of a woman's body humbles my ideas.

———————

Seduction: love yourself a little to be loved a lot. A woman's most beautiful makeup is passion.

It is when her youth begins to fade that a woman becomes increasingly moving.

———————

It is only aesthetic ghosts that make life possible.

Fashion is an incurable disease. As Metternich said, the greatest art is to endure.

All my life, I will remember my teenage years and my early youth in Algeria, that wonderful country. I don't feel like a *pied noir*. I feel like an Algerian — born Frenchman.
My memories carry me back so strongly to those wonderful days, to what Oran was at the time I was born. I can see that beautiful city, with its mix of races.

Algerians, French, Italians, Spaniards, all imprinting the city with their good humor, gaiety, their wild desire to live passionately.

My family, which was originally Alsatian, landed on that then-arid soil in 1870 in order not to live under the German occupation. In 1962, the same exodus in the opposite direction caused us to lose everything.

———————

A Naked Woman's body, which I must dress without inhibiting her natural freedom of movement; in a word, my trade is this naked woman's loving dialogue with all those spells cast by coiling fabric.

I would particularly like to thank:

Christian Baute, my producer and friend, who immediately understood the project, for his time, his trust and support throughout this adventure;

Frédéric Luzy, who believed in this project from the very beginning;

Dominique Deroche, without whom nothing would have been been possible. I would like to express my friendship and appreciation for her patience and her continuous support at every stage of the project;

My friend, Joël Brard, for his advice and friendship;

Caroline Champetier, for her meticulous photographic work;

Martine Giordano, for bringing all her intelligence and editing talent to the film;

James A. Fox, for his valuable attention throughout the long work of editing which he carried out with his usual talent and generosity ;

Xavier Barral, for the enthousiasm with which he welcomed the completed project;
Stéphane Cremer, and all the team at Atalante;

Marion Kalter, for her friendship and support;

Jacques Nassif, for listening to me and for his support;

Pauline Just, in spite of her silence;

Pierre Bergé, for his confidence.

I am particularly grateful to
Yves Saint Laurent et Pierre Bergé.

Thanks to
Annie Alter, Mireille Aranias, Danièle Arbid, Jean Barral, Didier Bogard, Annie Boulat, Marion de Brunhoff,
Patric Chiha, Edmonde Charles-Roux, Francine Dupraz, Marie-Christine Durand, Harun Farocki,
Jean-Marc Felzenszwalbe, Anne Flammand, Rachel Funaro, Jill Galliéni, Jean-Paul Gaultier, Nicole Gersen,
Françoise Giroud, Anna Glogowski, Yolande de Gourcuff, Valérie Guiter, Pierre Hanau, Dana Hastier,
Ruth Henry, Dagmar Jacobsen, Louisette Kahane, Georges Kiejman, Philippe Kholy, Nathalie Kreuther,
Catherine Lamour, Jean-Louis Langlois, Marie Lantier, Pascal Lebrun-Cordier, Augustin Legrand,
Nathalie Locatelli, Danièle Maisonnasse, Franck Mallet, Jacques Mandelbaum, Thomas de Mateïs,
Lucienne Mathieu-Saint-Laurent, Nadia Michel, Sellim Nassib, Dominique Païni, Philippe Pavans,
Catherine Poitevin, Jean-Philippe Pons, Christine Reisen, Anne Seuguin, Muriel Tohmé, Barbara Tubaro,
Michiko Yoshitake, Hanns Zischler.

I would like to thank
the House of Yves Saint Laurent Haute Couture:

Anne-Marie Muñoz, Loulou de la Falaise;

Catherine Gadala, Marie-Thérèse Herzog, Hélène de Ludinghausen, Paule Moninot, Audrey Secnazi,
Olivier Ségot, Elie Top, Danielle Vinmer;

Georgette Capelli, Jean-Pierre Derbord, Frédérique Desinde, Philippe Lesage, Colette Maciet,
Alain Marchais, Christelle Posada;

Nicole Dorier, Dorota Jop;

Elisa Charpentier, Virginie Laubie-Besse, Claude Mialaud;

Catherine Biro, Carlina Falucca, Christiane Lahaye;

Pascal Sittler;

Nieves Alvarez, Lavinia Birlandeanu, Laëtitia Casta, Lydia Korweva, Claire Lavigne, Amy Lemons,
Sabrina Magalhaes, Kewe Mar mamé, Suelen Pinho Monteiro, Mr Montex, Gérald Porscher,
Georgiana Roberston, Inga Savits, Lieke Smets, Amalia Vairelli, Bambi Van Leen, Triin Vellimsaar,
Jean-Luc Villeneuve, Dorotha Voj, Johana Zikova;

Caroline Benguigui, Aurore Beyaert, Rosana Konofalski, Poly Tuy Studio;

Sophie Cottat, Jacques Forest, Pascale Léautey, Myriam Rollin;

Laurent Chapus, Marie-Laurence Gimeno, Danièle Leclercq-Jabelot;

Charles Azzopardi, Faiza Chergui, Christian Forel et son équipe, Jean-Pierre Guihard, Maria Matos,
Augusto Ribeiro, Nadège Rivalan, Emmanuel Robin, Muriel Silva, Paul Valentin;

Laurence Neveu, Hector Pascual, Jean-Philippe Pons, Frédéric-Romain Verdure.

My work would not have been possible without the daily participation of
Odile Aguerre, Takako Akasu, Aziz Alici, Gérard Avakian, Cemil Avcikara, Pierrette Belhassein,
Brigitte Benoist, Jeanine Bertranet, Mehmet Beydili, Béatrice de Boissy, Patrick Bordeaux, Danielle Boyard,
Dominique Brillard, Anita Brissonnet, Dominique Bugnez, Evelyne Buvat, Francine Buvat, Cahit Celik,
Nisan Celik, Florence Chehet, Claudine Chemin, Béatrice Chevillard, Fatima Chouhada-Nouradi,
Sophie Chung, Maria-Isabel Clamote, Eliane Clarion, Chrissi Cocher, Celsa Correas, Chrystele Coudert,
Anne Daphniet, Nicole Debats, Sophie Delamotte, Lucette Demange, Marlène Devesches, Nicole Dietrich,
Antony Dilmen, Eliane, Muriel Febve, Véronique Ferré, Marc Flury, Margot Gaestka,
Maria-Carmen Garaicoechea, Céline Gegousse, Danielle Genipa, Irène Gerhardt, Luc Godmuse,
Maria Gonzalez-Paredes, Marie Claire Guillemain, Renetta Hildevert, Demirdelen Ismail, Monique Jamet,
Bayram Kaya, Méhmet Kemikler, Omer Kilinc, Dominique Kokai, Nevsat Kumas, Isabelle Laguette,
Catherine Lainé, Athanasia Lambert, Rosine Lambert, Arnaud Lance, Eric Lantoine, Rose-Marie Lhermite,
Brigitte Lenoir, Cesar Lombardo, Lunungu Langa, Marinelle, Josepha Meslet Martinez, Jean Melkonian,
Emmanuelle Miramand, Jeannine Moine, Laurence Morin, Rania Mouhoubi, Habib Mtibaa, Olivier Paulhac,
Hyasmine Pecquet, Josette Peltier, Martine Perez, Jacqueline Pernold, Claudine Pernot, Rosario Pla,
Nicole Potulhy, Marie-Christine Priam, Catherine Regnier, Marcelle Rouget, Christine Roulet,
Lydie Rousseau, Edith Ribette, Halil Sahan, Semsettin Sahbaz, Ramazan Sahin, Joelle Santin,
Françoise Satabin, Jacqueline Smeyers, Colette Stralen, Mireille Thiolière, Waltraud Tillakaratna,
Kesone Tran Rusen-Esref Yazan, Amphaphone Vongsouvan, and "Moujik" the dog.

A huge thank you to everybody who contributed to the making of this film
through their presence or participation.

Conception and graphics
Atalante / Paris, France
(33) 1 48 05 65 30 / atalante@atalante-paris.fr

Art editing
James A. Fox, David Teboul, Xavier Barral, Anne Chevry

English translation
Alexandra Bonfante-Warren and Molly Stevens

Photographic reproductions
Eric Guillot

All the color images in this book were taken directly
from David Teboul's HD cam film.
The processing and color grading of these digital images
were carried out by Le Studio, Paris in close collaboration
with Alain Mouchère, who made the trial print on his presses
at Savigny-sur-Orge (4M Impressions,France).
The last color retouching before printing was carried out
by Atalante /Paris,with the kind assistance of Daniel Regard.

Photographic credits :
1, 2, 3, 4, 5, 6, 7, 8, 9, 10, 11, 15, Yves Saint Laurent private collection.
12, 13, 14, 16, All rights reserved.
17, David Teboul.

Harry N. Abrams, Inc.
100 Fifth Avenue
New York, N.Y. 10011
www.abramsbooks.com

Abrams is a subsidiary of